Color By Number Adult Coloring Book

This Adult Color By Number Book belongs to:

_____

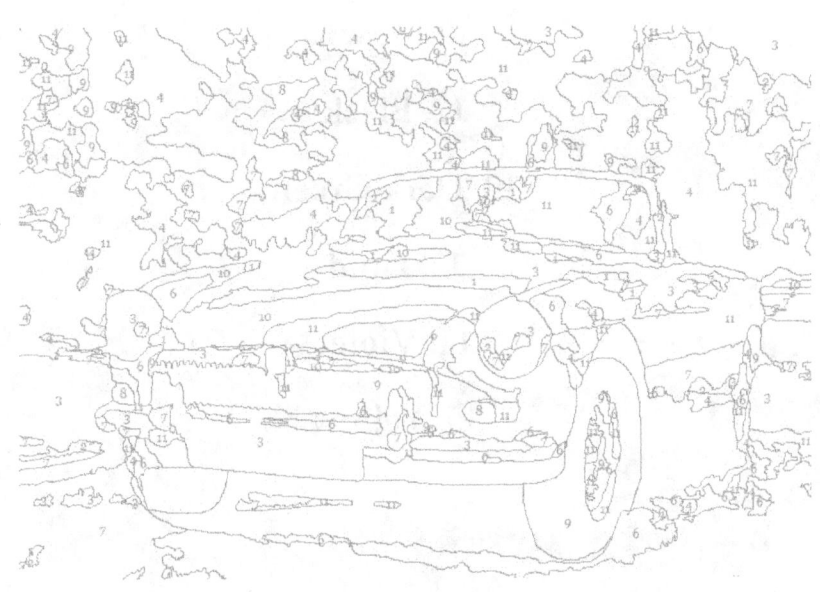

1. Red

2. Green

3. Blue

4. Pink

5. Purple

6. Light Blue

7. Light Green

8. Orange

9. Dark Red

10.Brown

11. Black

12. Dark Green

13. Gold

14. Violet

15. Yellow

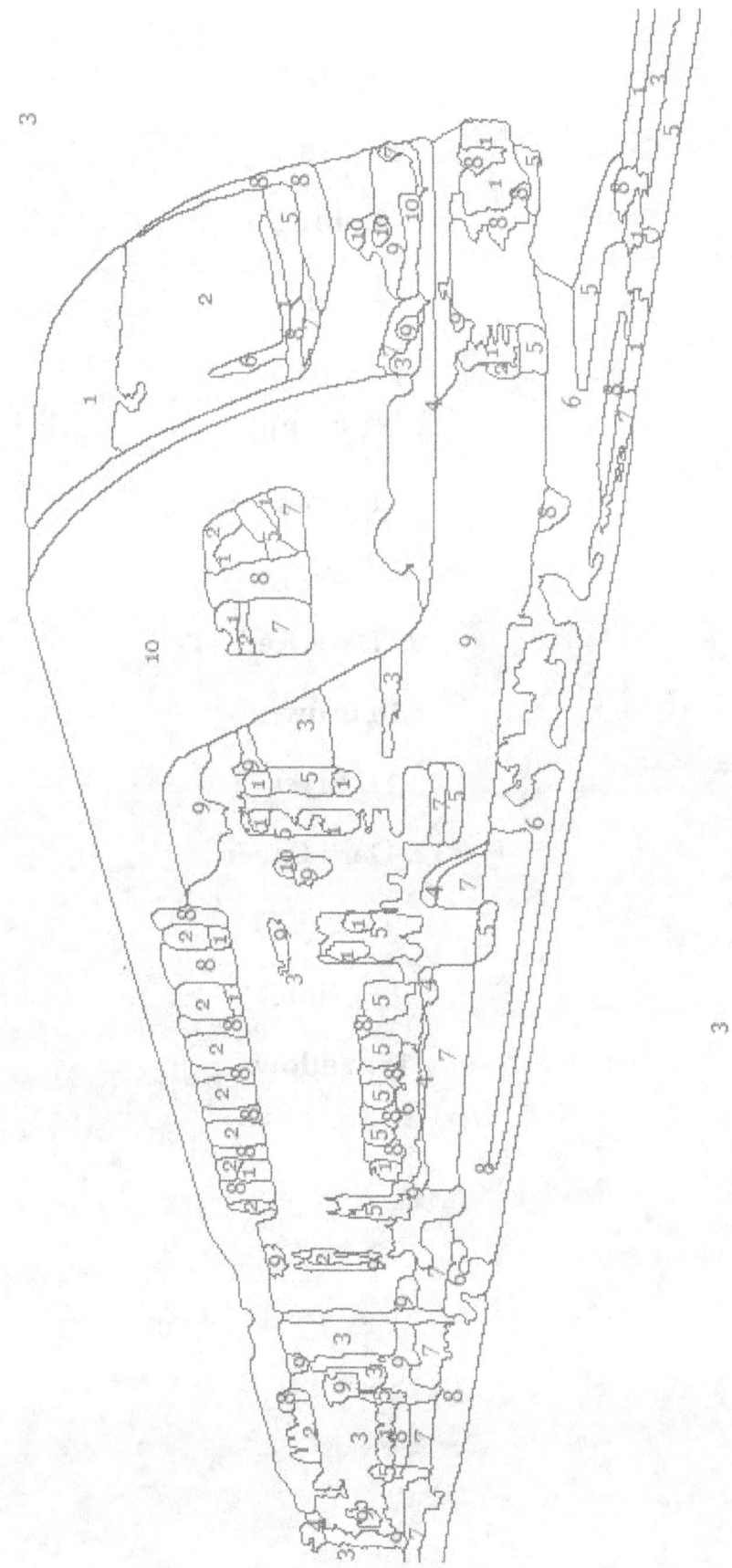

1. Red

2. Green

3. Blue

4. Pink

5. Purple

6. Light Blue

7. Light Green

8. Orange

9. Dark Red

10. Brown

11. Black

12. Dark Green

13. Gold

14. Violet

15. Yellow

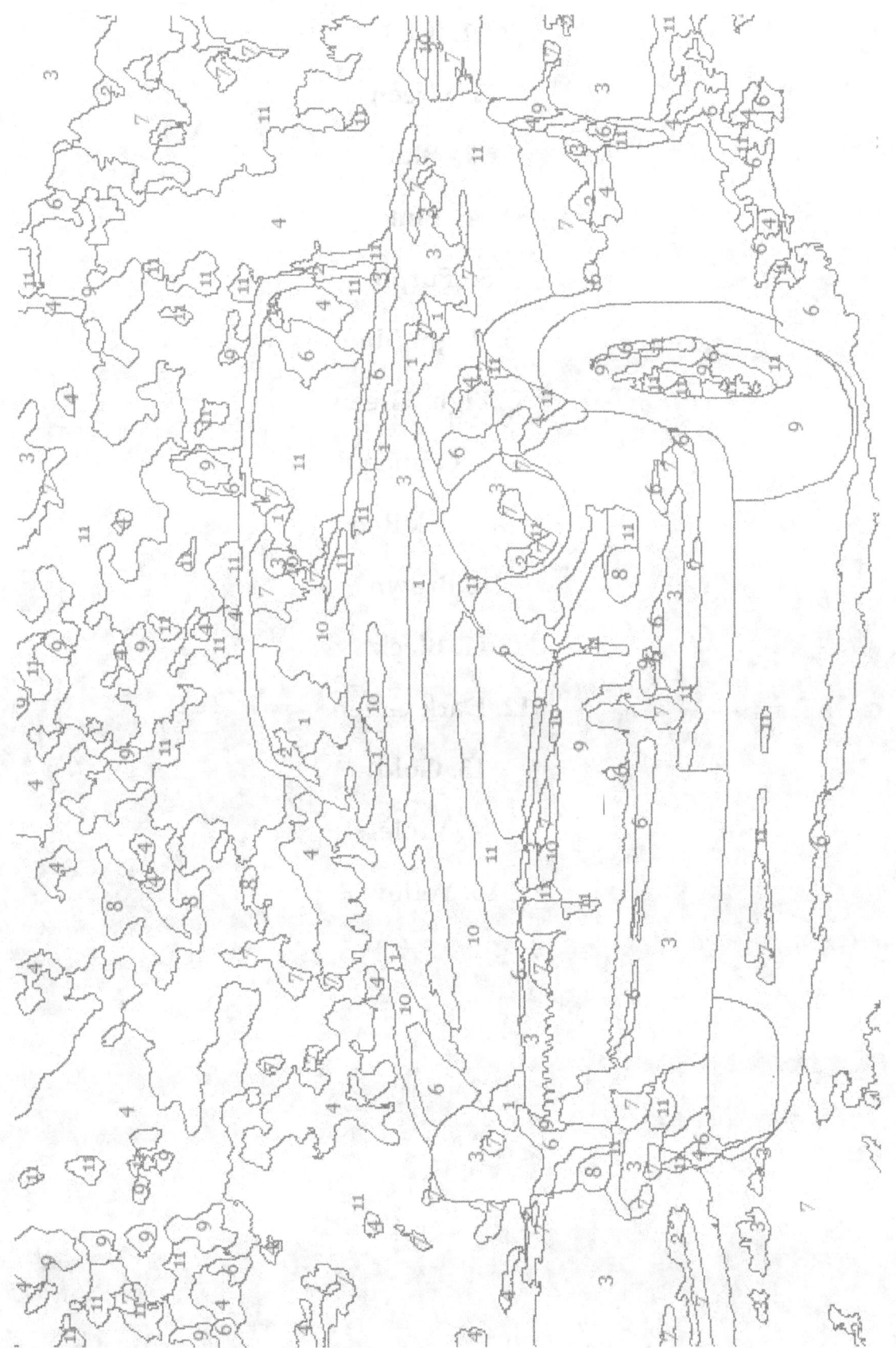

1. Red

2. Green

3. Blue

4. Pink

5. Purple

6. Light Blue

7. Light Green

8. Orange

9. Dark Red

10. Brown

11. Black

12. Dark Green

13. Gold

14. Violet

15. Yellow

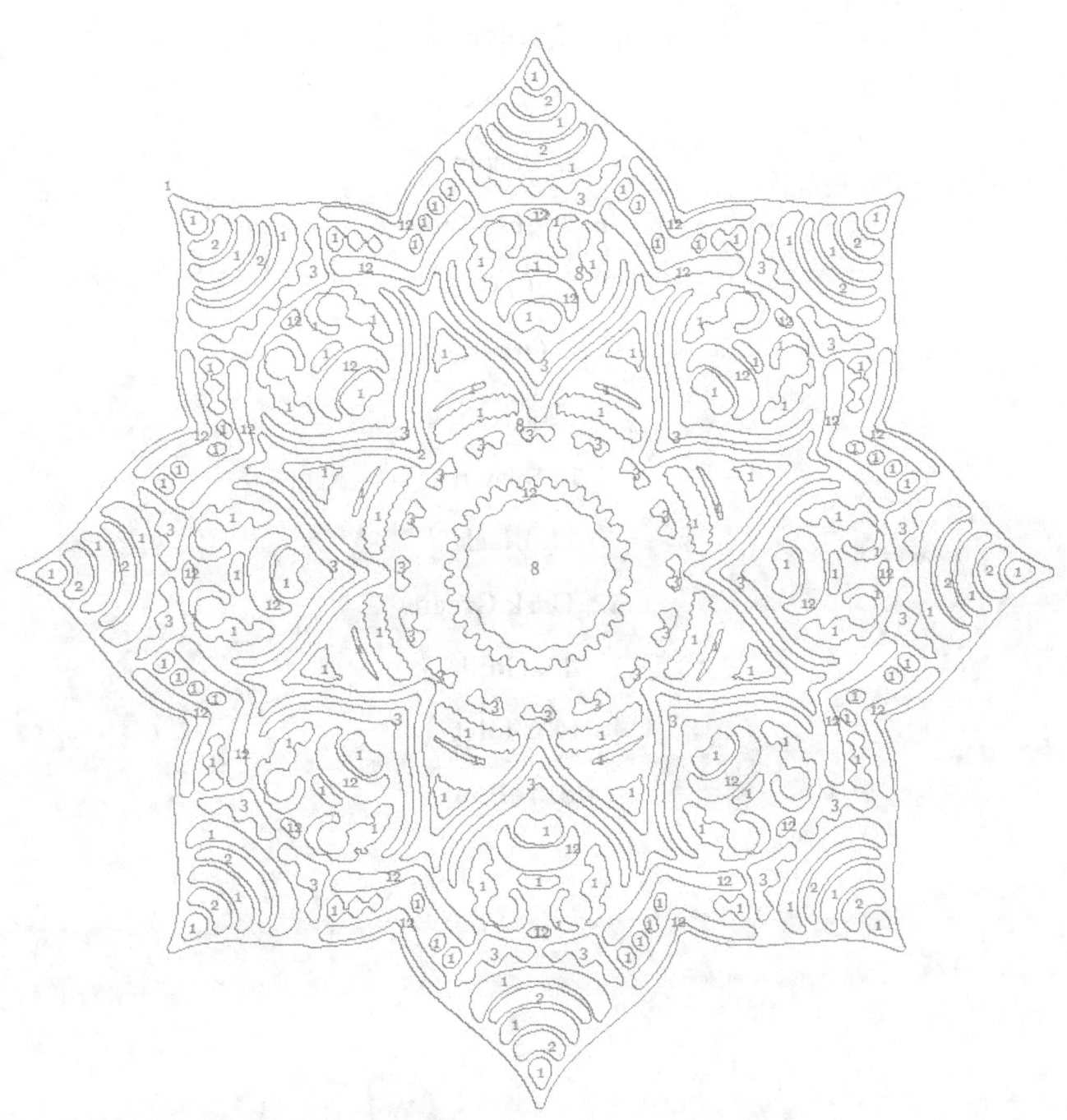

1. Red

2. Green

3. Blue

4. Pink

5. Purple

6. Light Blue

7. Light Green

8. Orange

9. Dark Red

10. Brown

11. Black

12. Dark Green

13. Gold

14. Violet

15. Yellow

1. Red

2. Green

3. Blue

4. Pink

5. Purple

6. Light Blue

7. Light Green

8. Orange

9. Dark Red

10. Brown

11. Black

12. Dark Green

13. Gold

14. Violet

15. Yellow

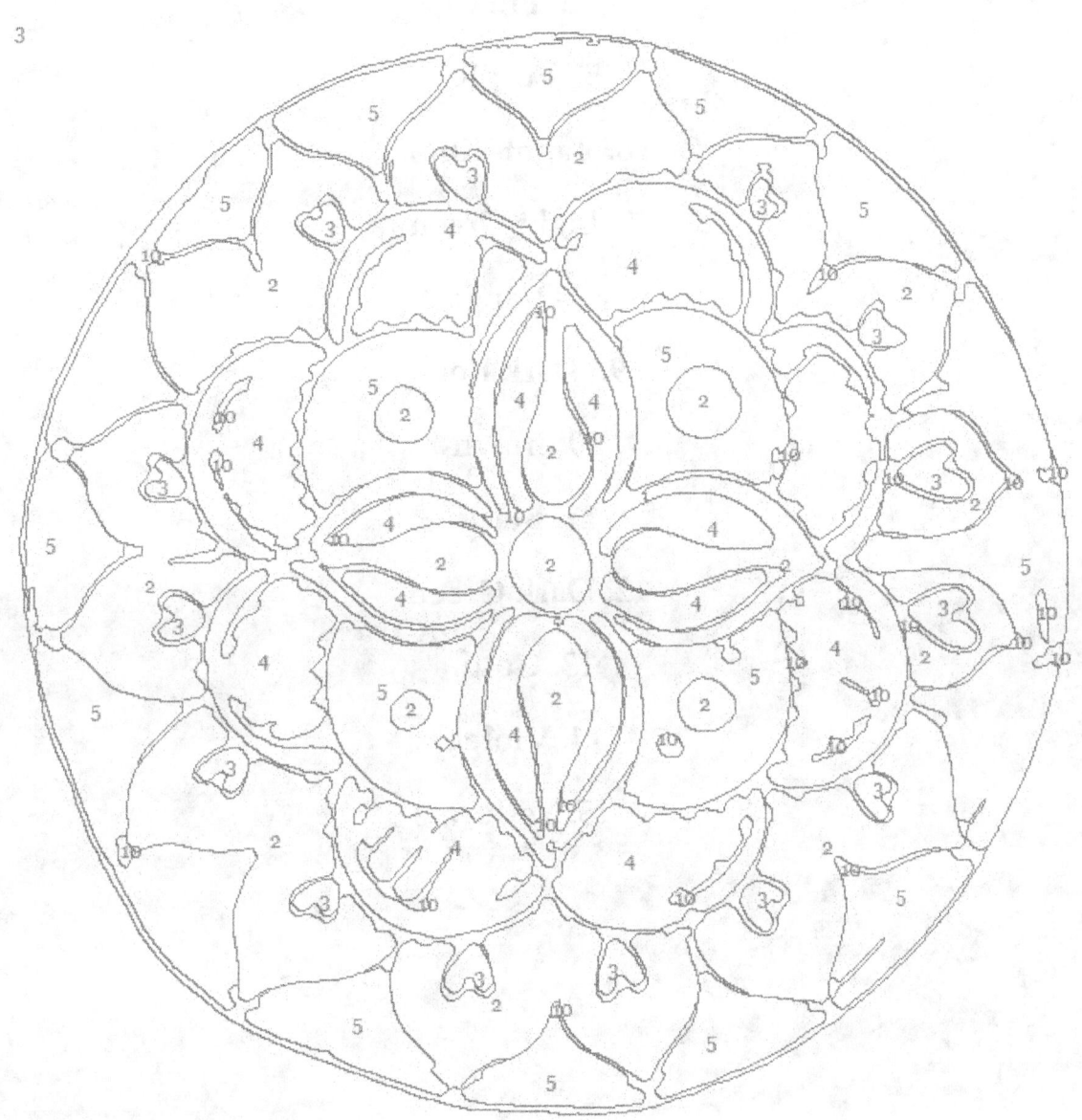

1. Red

2. Green

3. Blue

4. Pink

5. Purple

6. Light Blue

7. Light Green

8. Orange

9. Dark Red

10. Brown

11. Black

12. Dark Green

13. Gold

14. Violet

15. Yellow

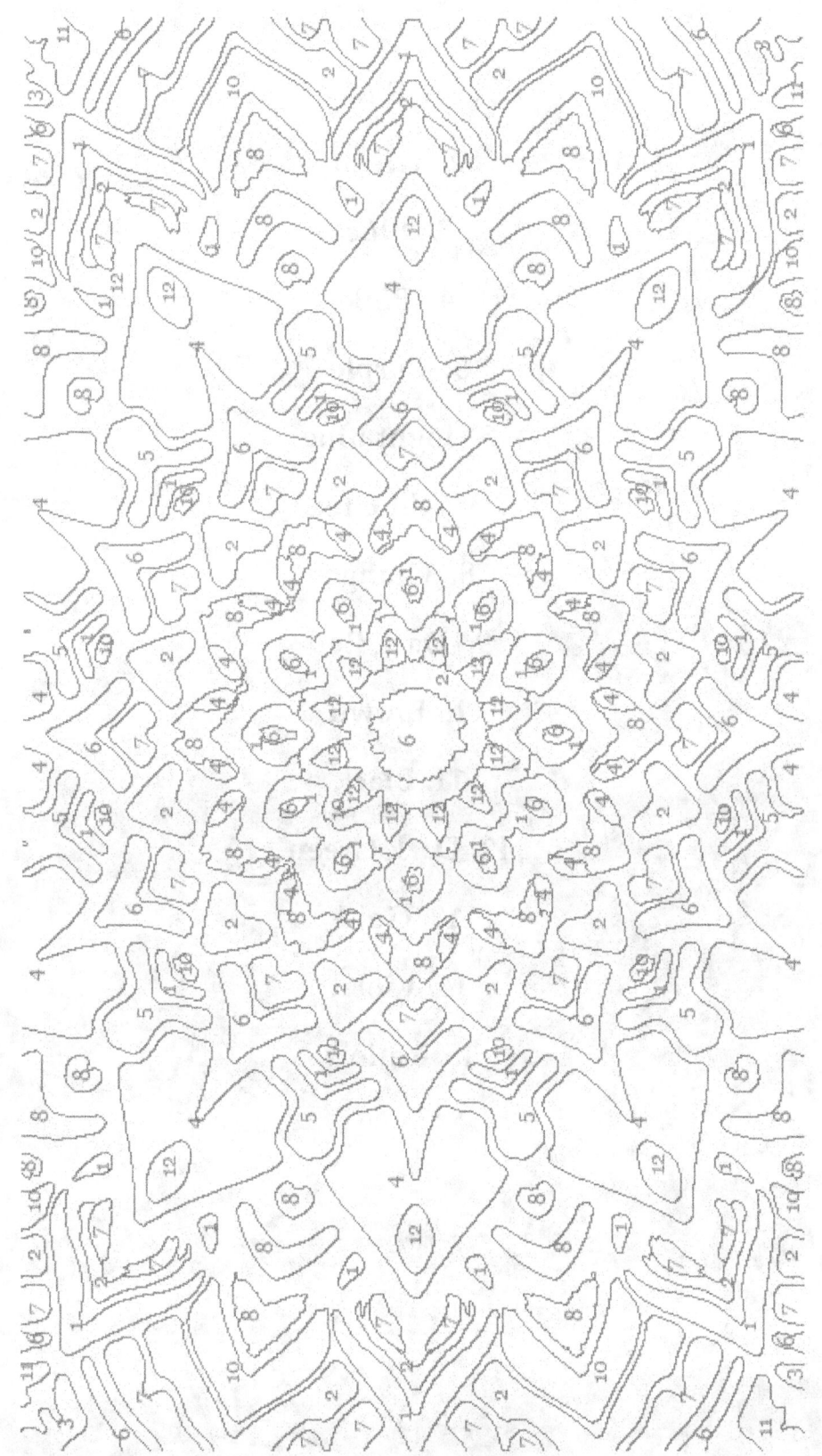

1. Red

2. Green

3. Blue

4. Pink

5. Purple

6. Light Blue

7. Light Green

8. Orange

9. Dark Red

10. Brown

11. Black

12. Dark Green

13. Gold

14. Violet

15. Yellow

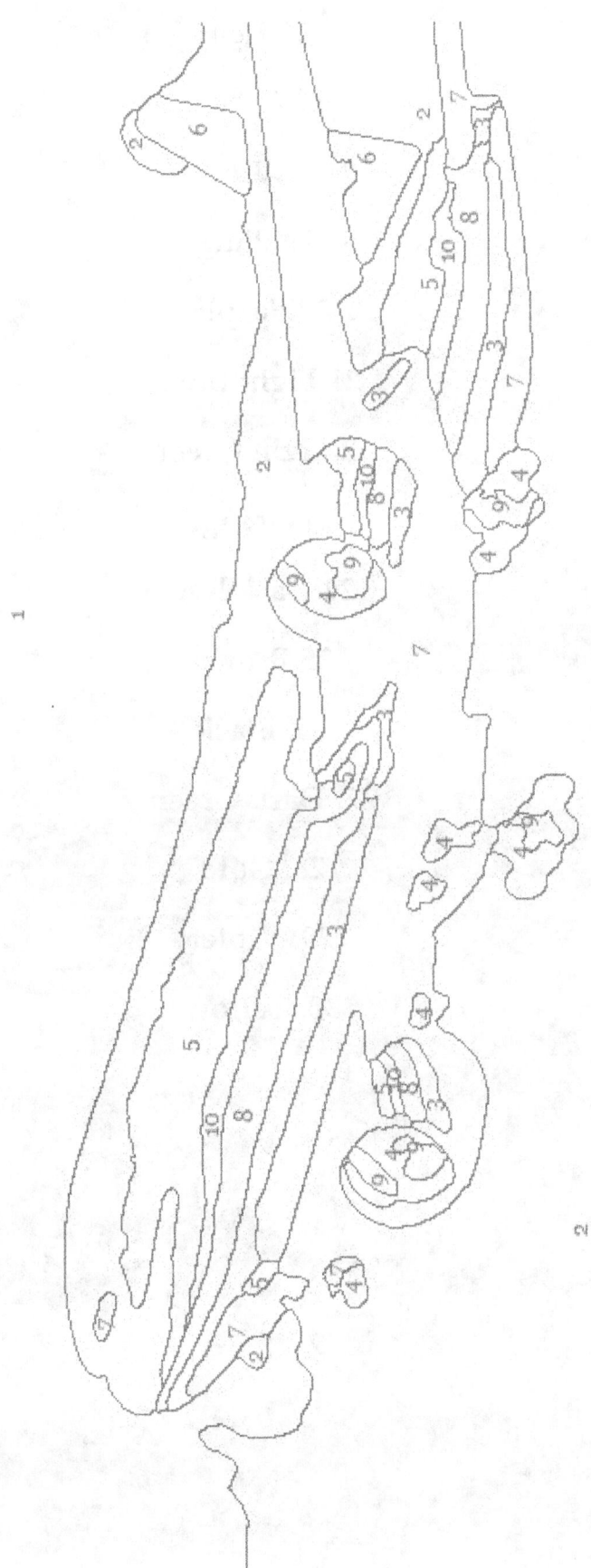

16. Red

17. Green

18. Blue

19. Pink

20. Purple

21. Light Blue

22. Light Green

23. Orange

24. Dark Red

25. Brown

26. Black

27. Dark Green

28. Gold

29. Violet

30. Yellow

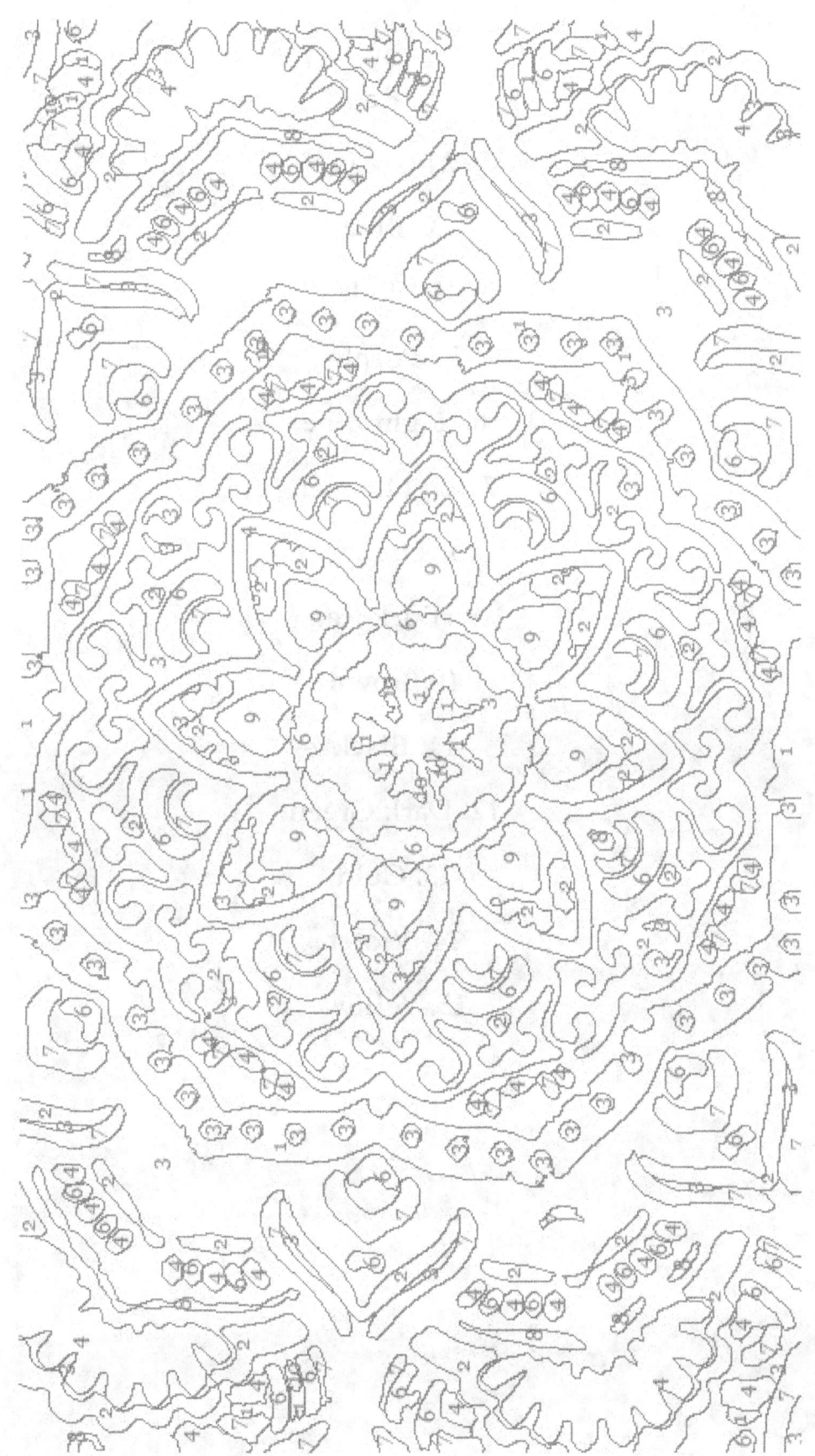

1. Red

2. Green

3. Blue

4. Pink

5. Purple

6. Light Blue

7. Light Green

8. Orange

9. Dark Red

10. Brown

11. Black

12. Dark Green

13. Gold

14. Violet

15. Yellow

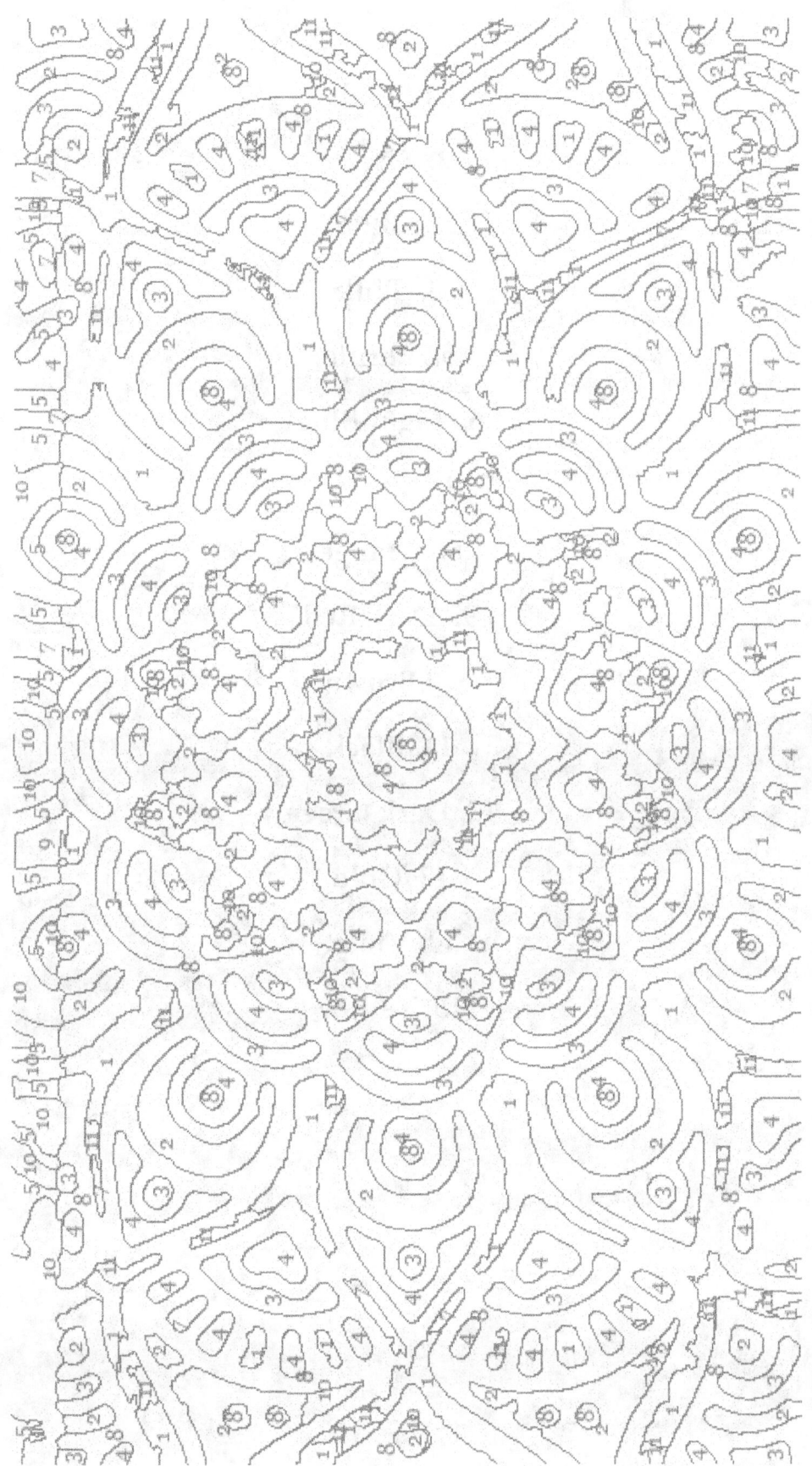

1. Red

2. Green

3. Blue

4. Pink

5. Purple

6. Light Blue

7. Light Green

8. Orange

9. Dark Red

10. Brown

11. Black

12. Dark Green

13. Gold

14. Violet

15. Yellow

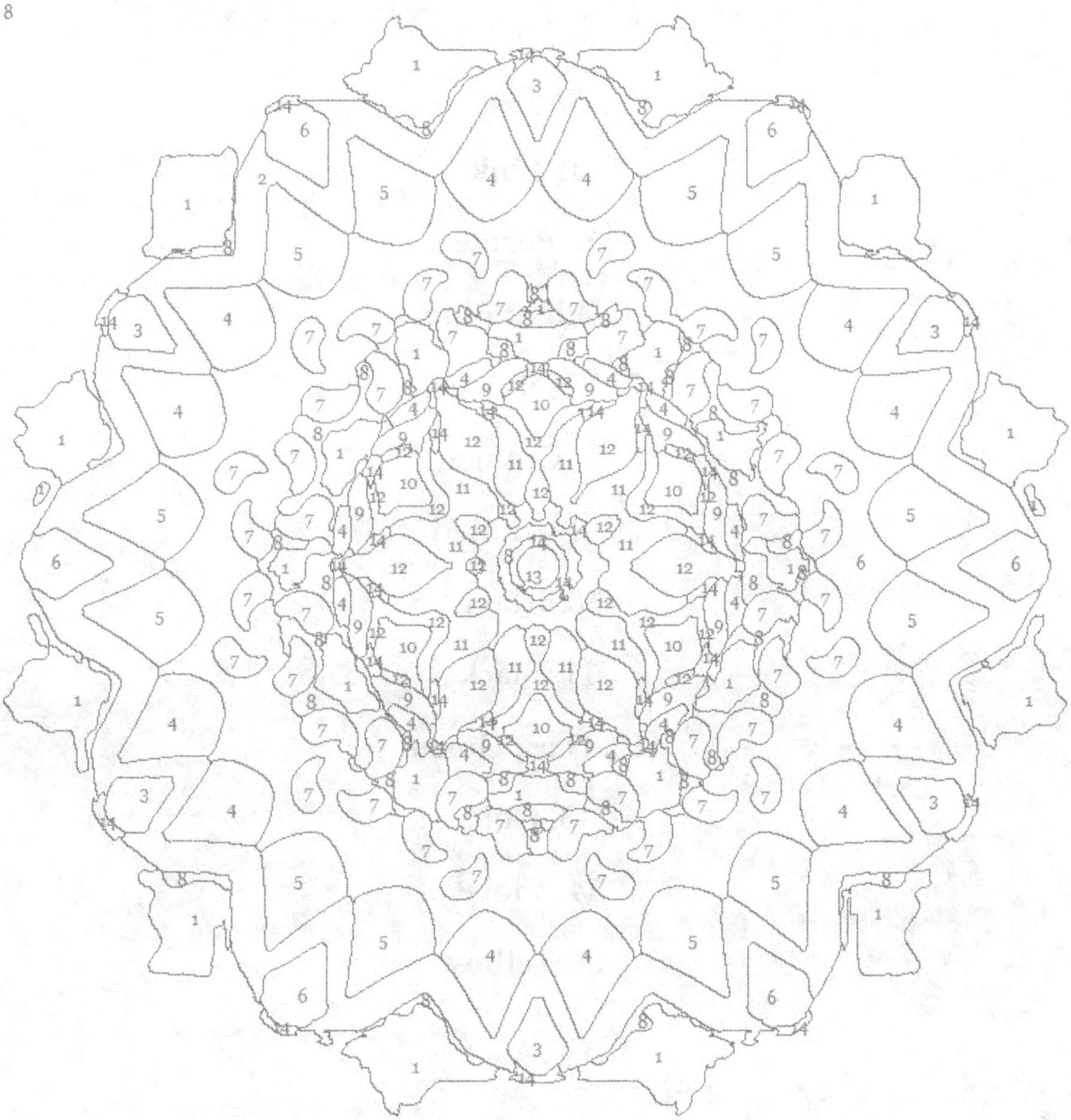

1. Red

2. Green

3. Blue

4. Pink

5. Purple

6. Light Blue

7. Light Green

8. Orange

9. Dark Red

10. Brown

11. Black

12. Dark Green

13. Gold

14. Violet

15. Yellow

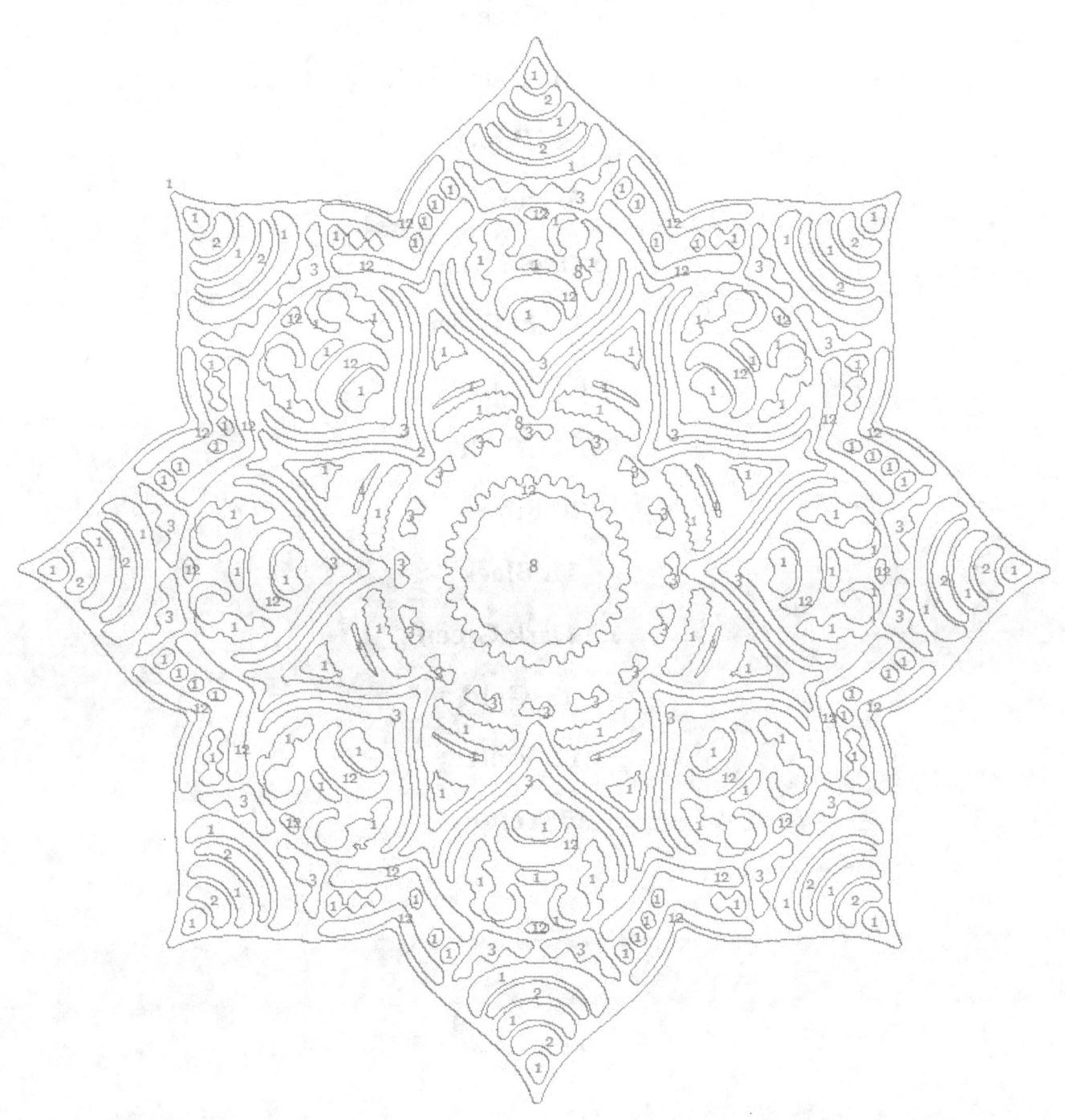

1. Red

2. Green

3. Blue

4. Pink

5. Purple

6. Light Blue

7. Light Green

8. Orange

9. Dark Red

10. Brown

11. Black

12. Dark Green

13. Gold

14. Violet

15. Yellow

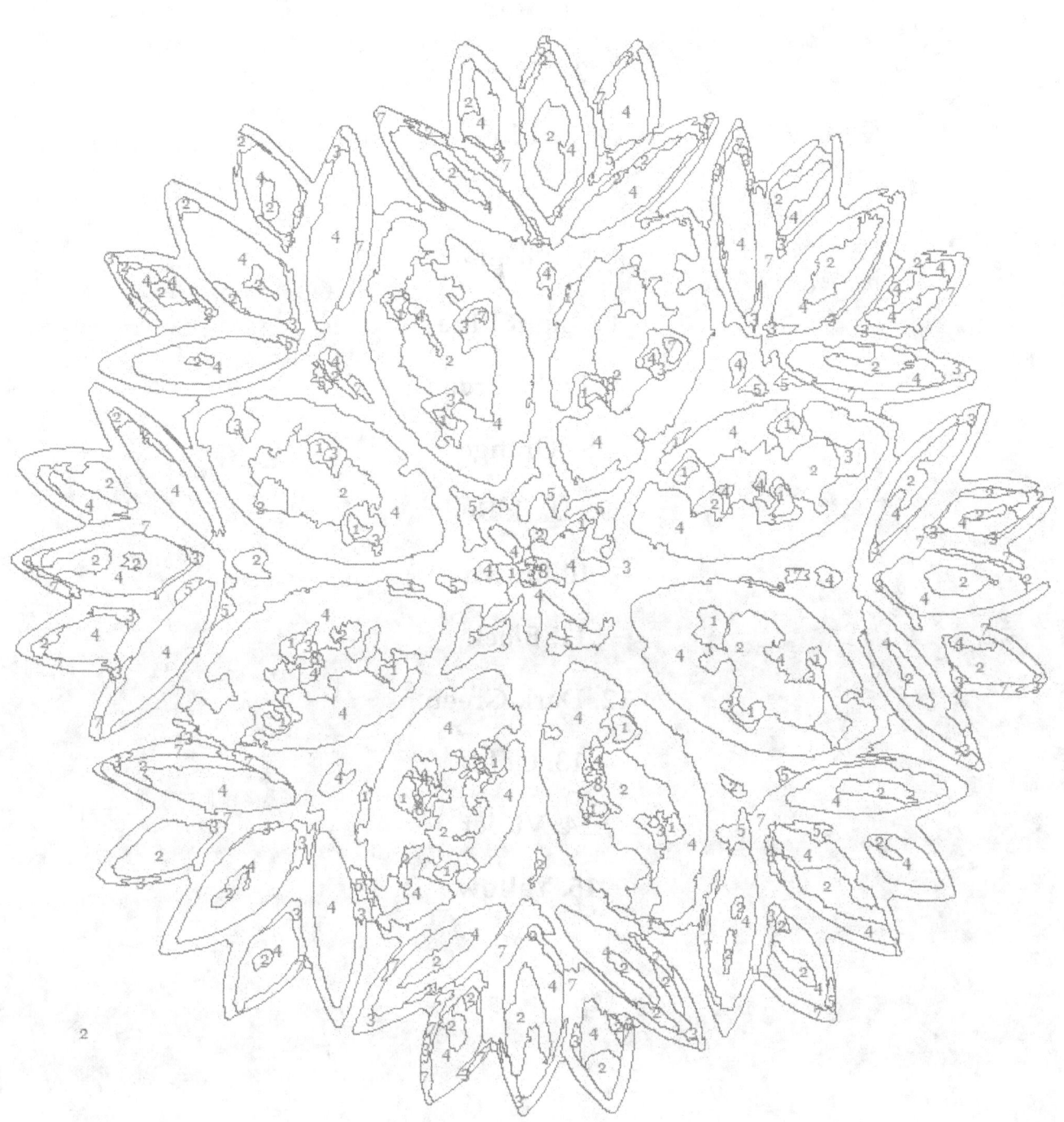

1. Red

2. Green

3. Blue

4. Pink

5. Purple

6. Light Blue

7. Light Green

8. Orange

9. Dark Red

10. Brown

11. Black

12. Dark Green

13. Gold

14. Violet

15. Yellow

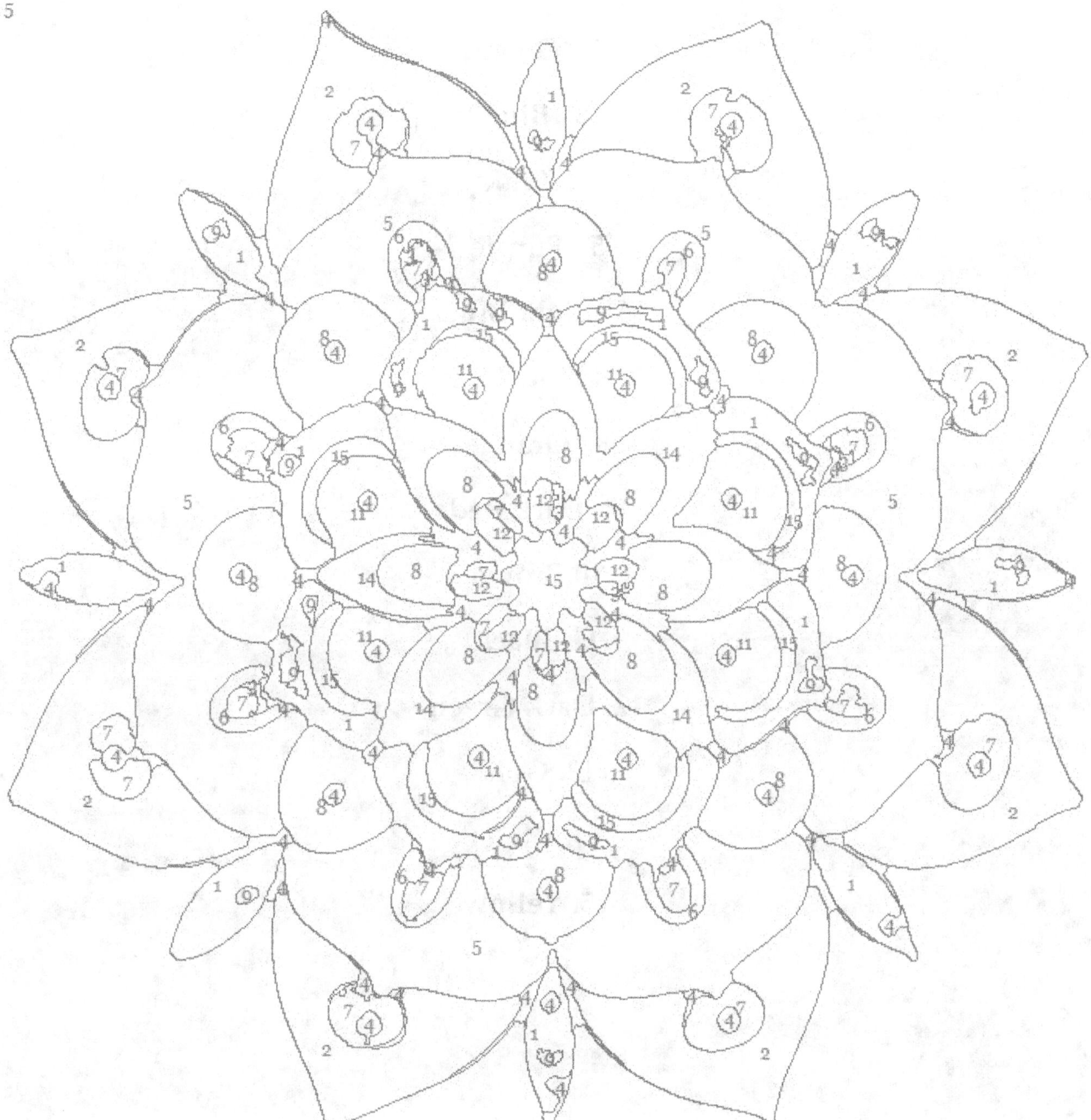

1. Red

2. Green

3. Blue

4. Pink

5. Purple

6. Light Blue

7. Light Green

8. Orange

9. Dark Red

10. Brown

11. Black

12. Dark Green

13. Gold

14. Violet

15. Yellow

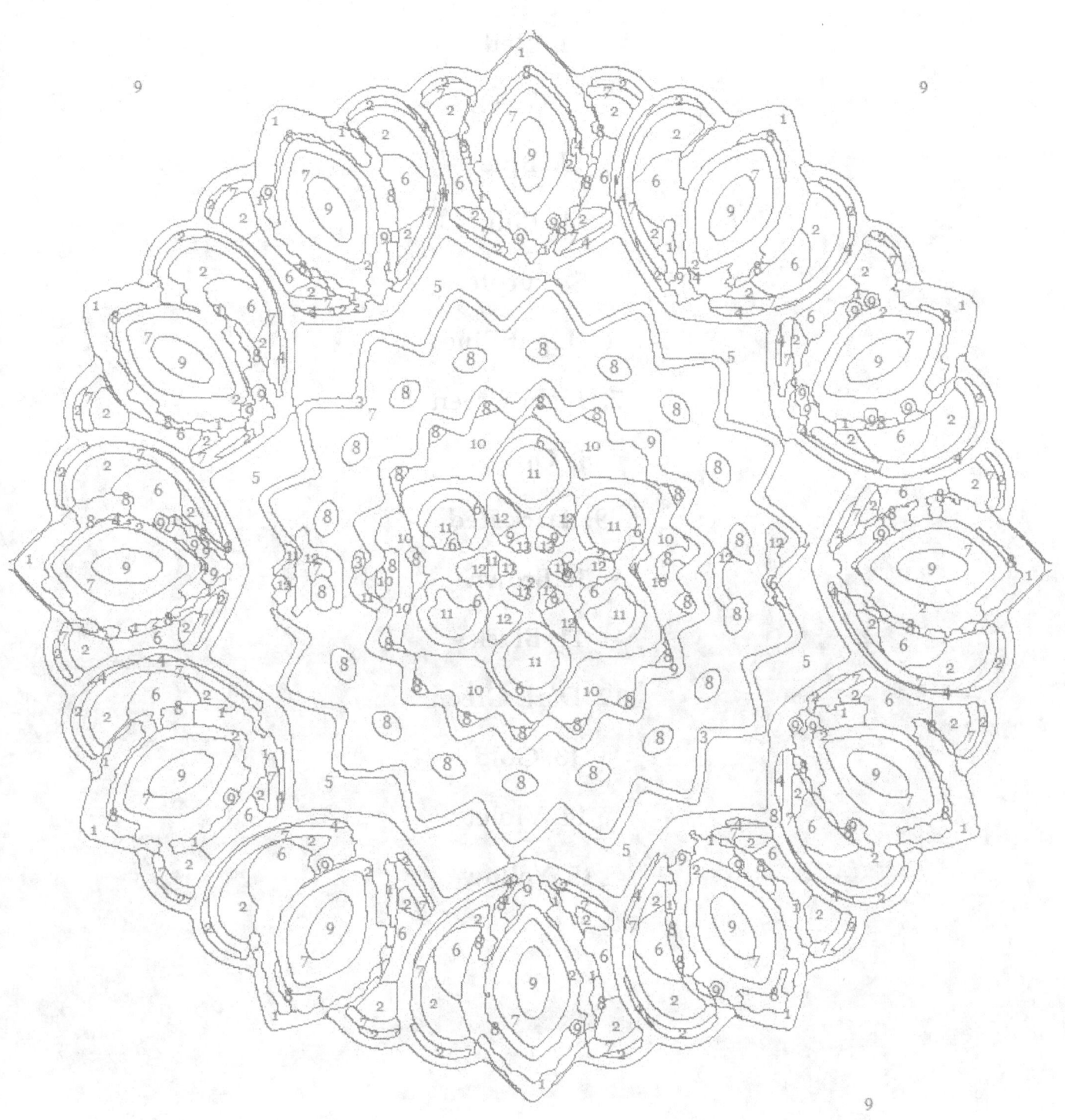

1. Red

2. Green

3. Blue

4. Pink

5. Purple

6. Light Blue

7. Light Green

8. Orange

9. Dark Red

10. Brown

11. Black

12. Dark Green

13. Gold

14. Violet

15. Yellow

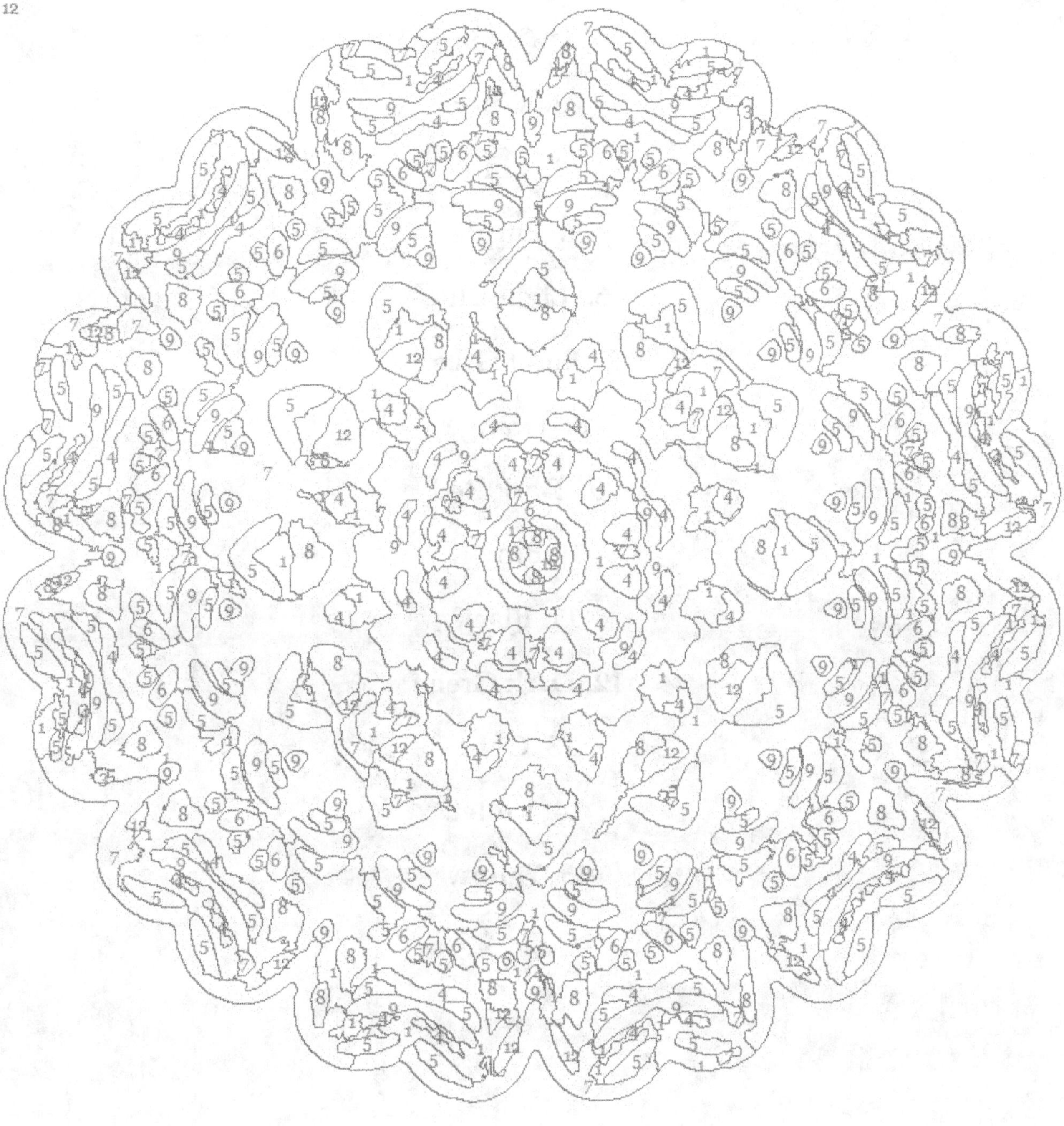

1. Red

2. Green

3. Blue

4. Pink

5. Purple

6. Light Blue

7. Light Green

8. Orange

9. Dark Red

10. Brown

11. Black

12. Dark Green

13. Gold

14. Violet

15. Yellow

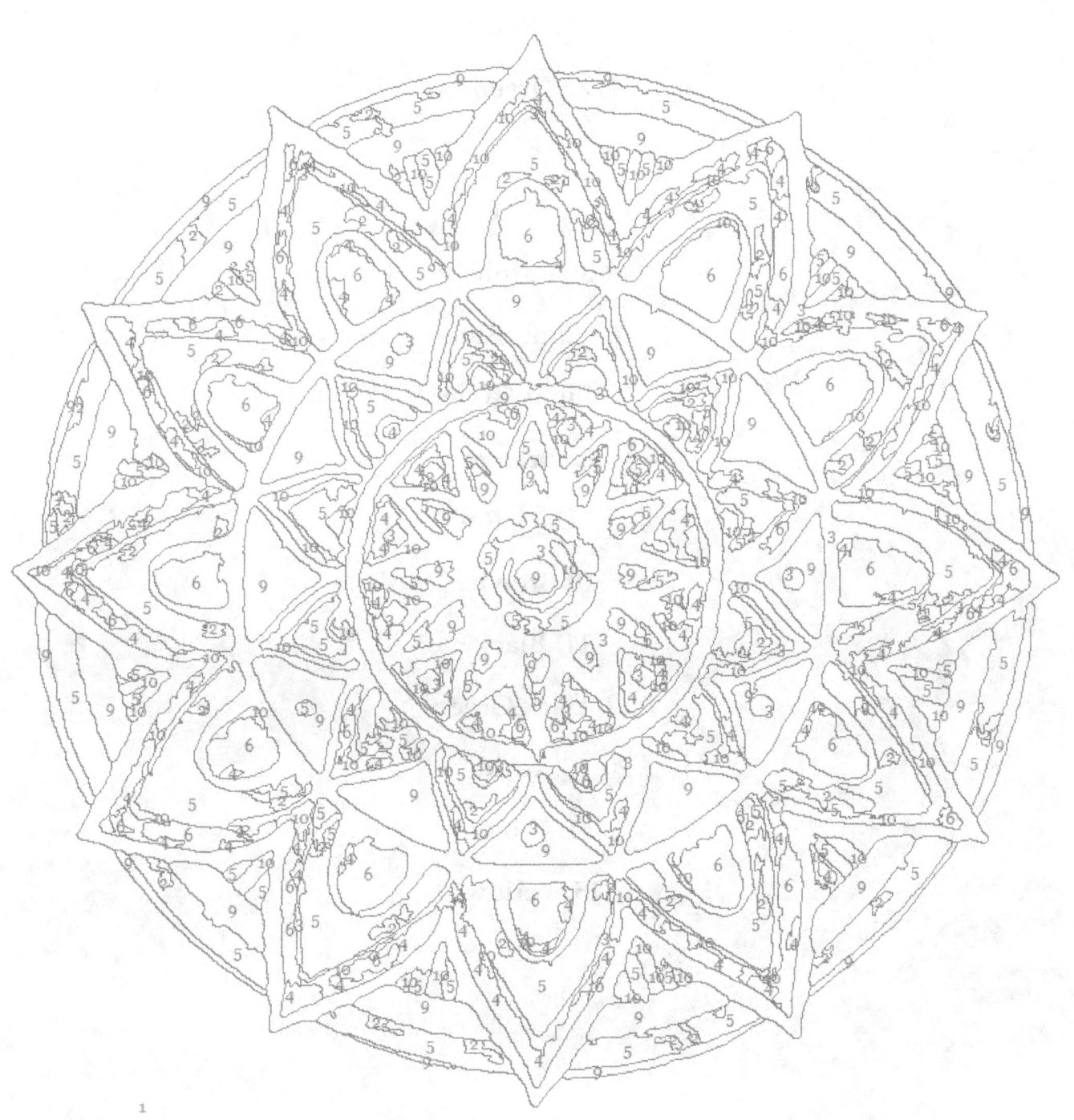

1

1. Red

2. Green

3. Blue

4. Pink

5. Purple

6. Light Blue

7. Light Green

8. Orange

9. Dark Red

10. Brown

11. Black

12. Dark Green

13. Gold

14. Violet

15. Yellow

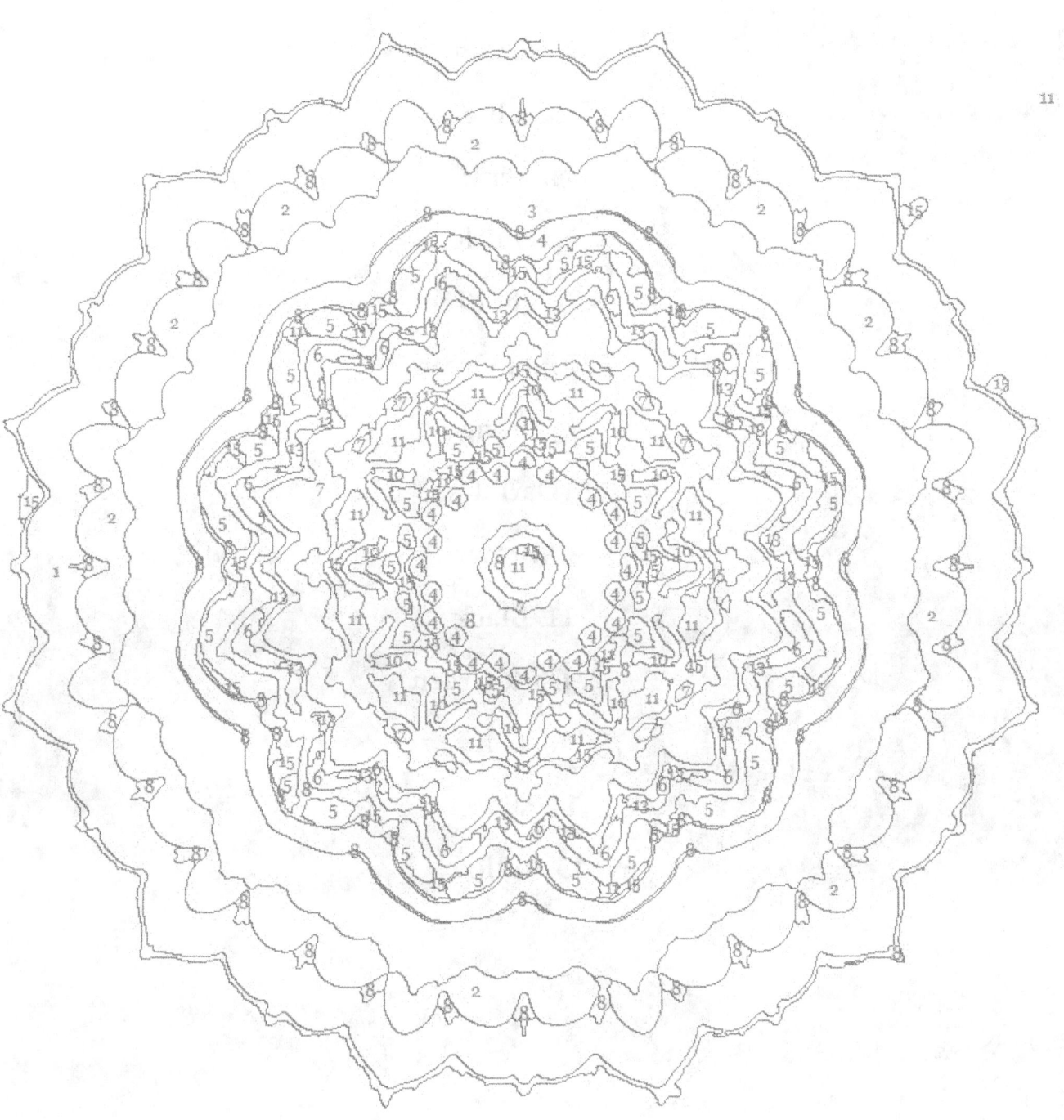

1. Red

2. Green

3. Blue

4. Pink

5. Purple

6. Light Blue

7. Light Green

8. Orange

9. Dark Red

10. Brown

11. Black

12. Dark Green

13. Gold

14. Violet

15. Yellow

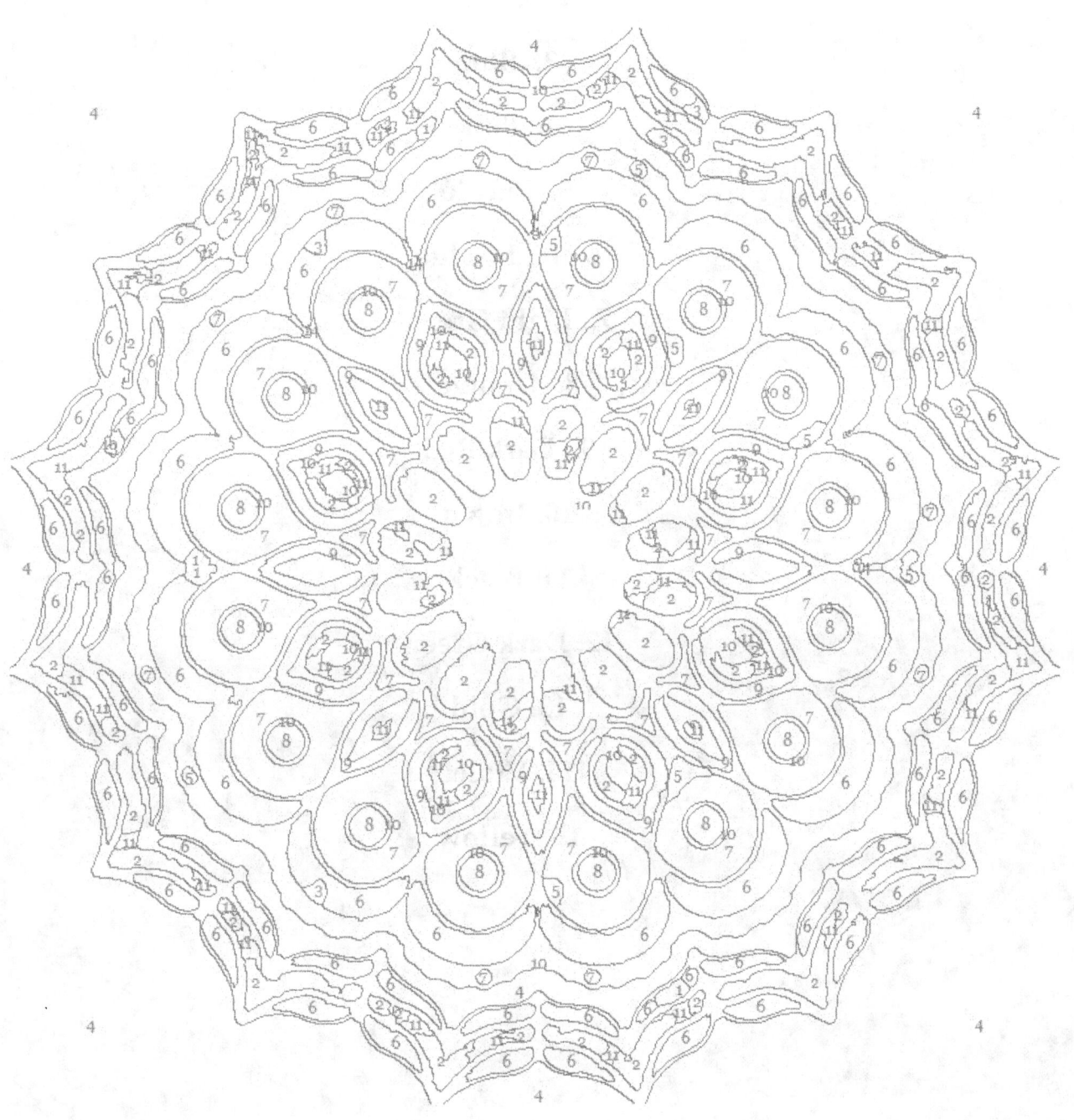

1. Red

2. Green

3. Blue

4. Pink

5. Purple

6. Light Blue

7. Light Green

8. Orange

9. Dark Red

10. Brown

11. Black

12. Dark Green

13. Gold

14. Violet

15. Yellow

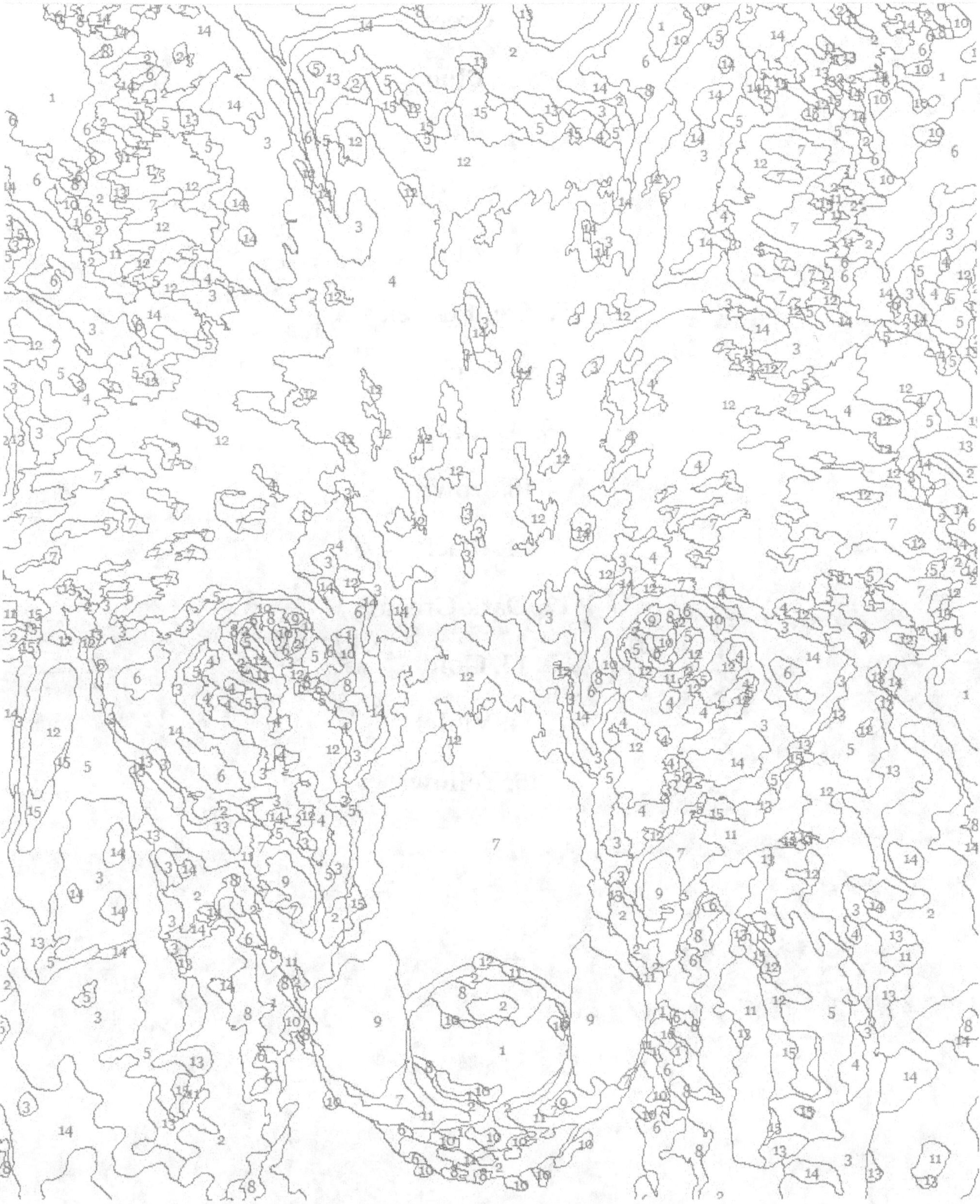

1. Red

2. Green

3. Blue

4. Pink

5. Purple

6. Light Blue

7. Light Green

8. Orange

9. Dark Red

10. Brown

11. Black

12. Dark Green

13. Gold

14. Violet

15. Yellow

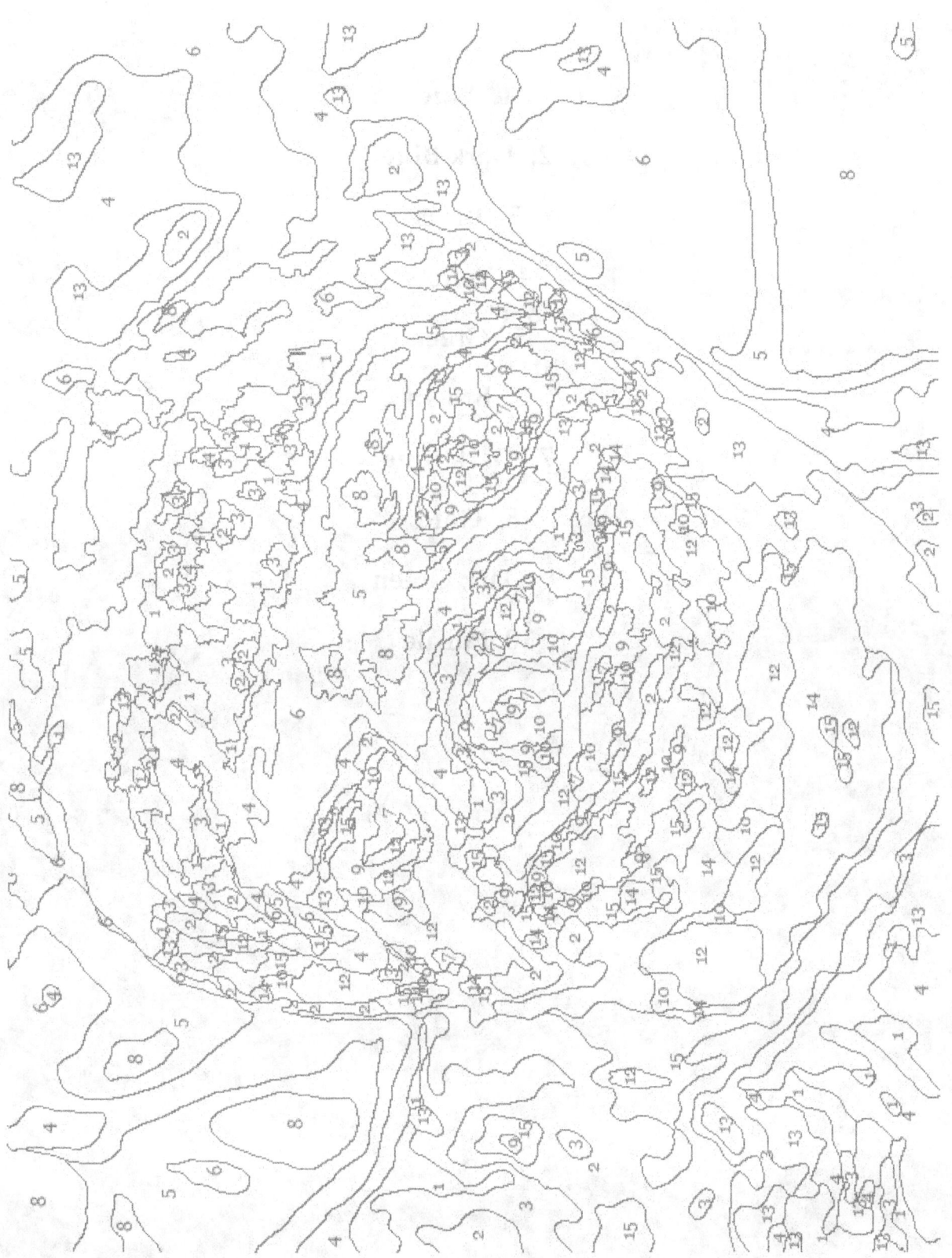

1. Blue

2. Dark Blue

3. Black

4. Yellow

5. Green

6. Brown

7. Dark Blue

8. Gold

9. Dark Green

10. Purple

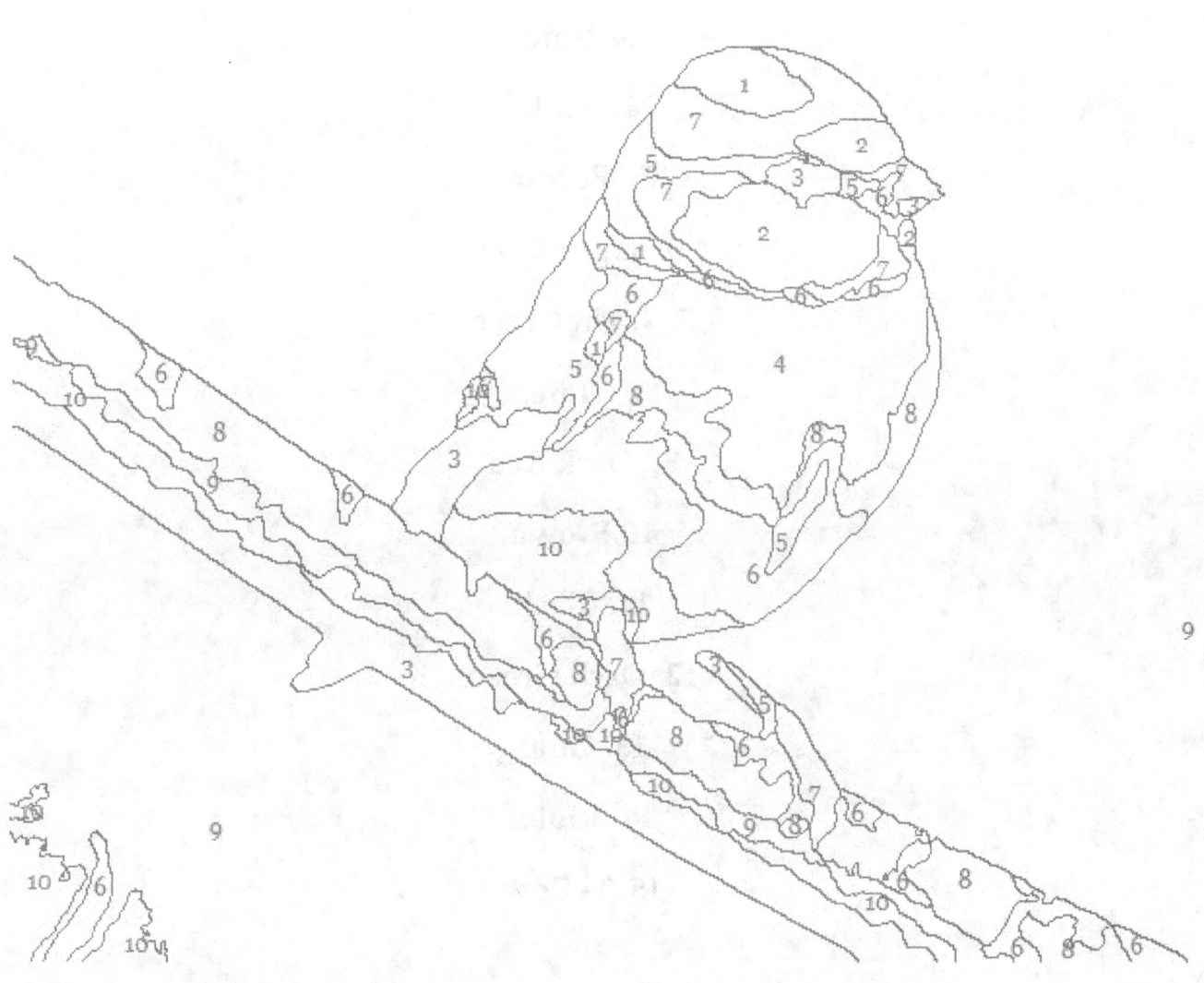

1. Red

2. Green

3. Blue

4. Pink

5. Purple

6. Light Blue

7. Light Green

8. Orange

9. Dark Red

10. Brown

11. Black

12. Dark Green

13. Gold

14. Violet

15. Yellow

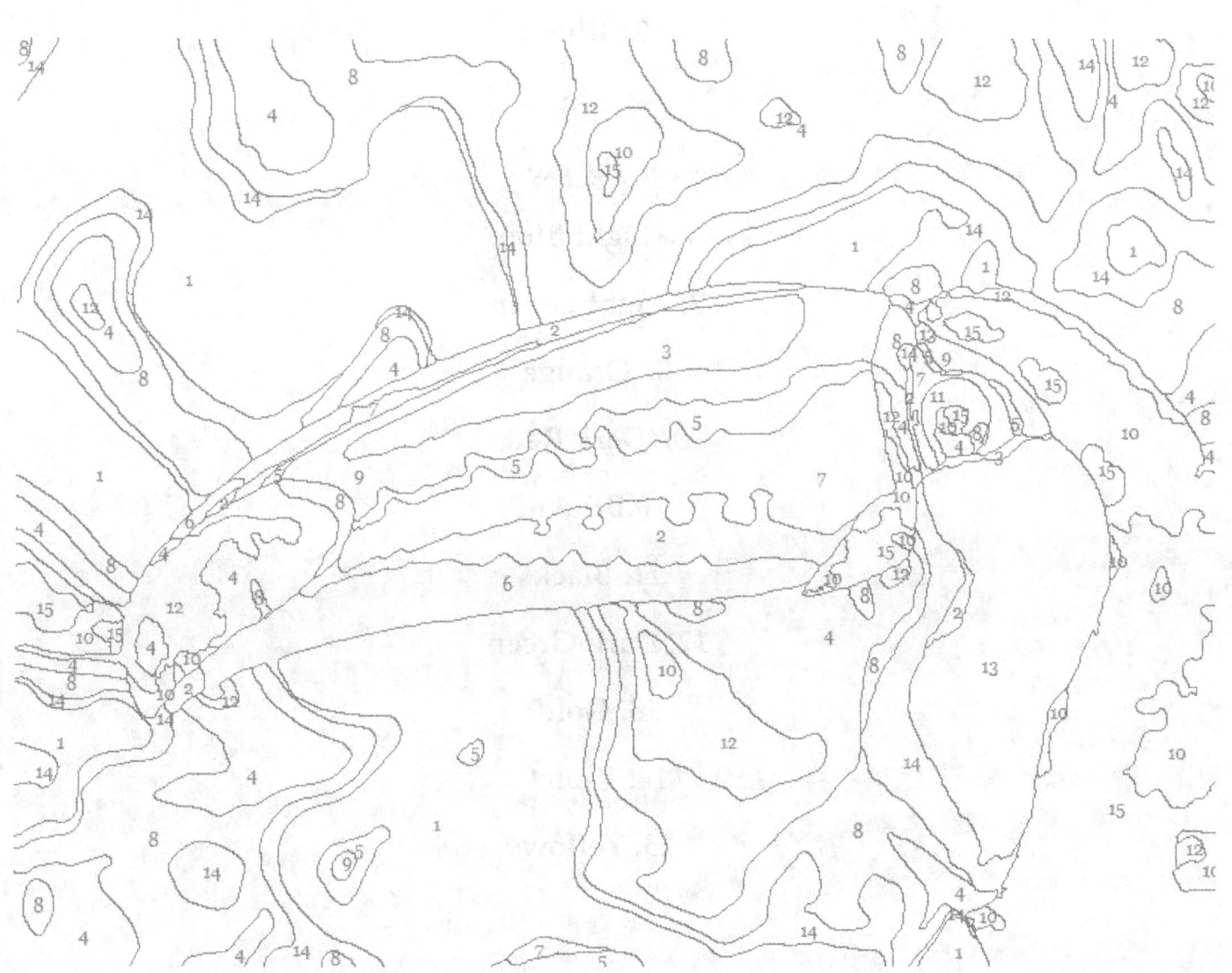

1. Red

2. Green

3. Blue

4. Pink

5. Purple

6. Light Blue

7. Light Green

8. Orange

9. Dark Red

10. Brown

11. Black

12. Dark Green

13. Gold

14. Violet

15. Yellow

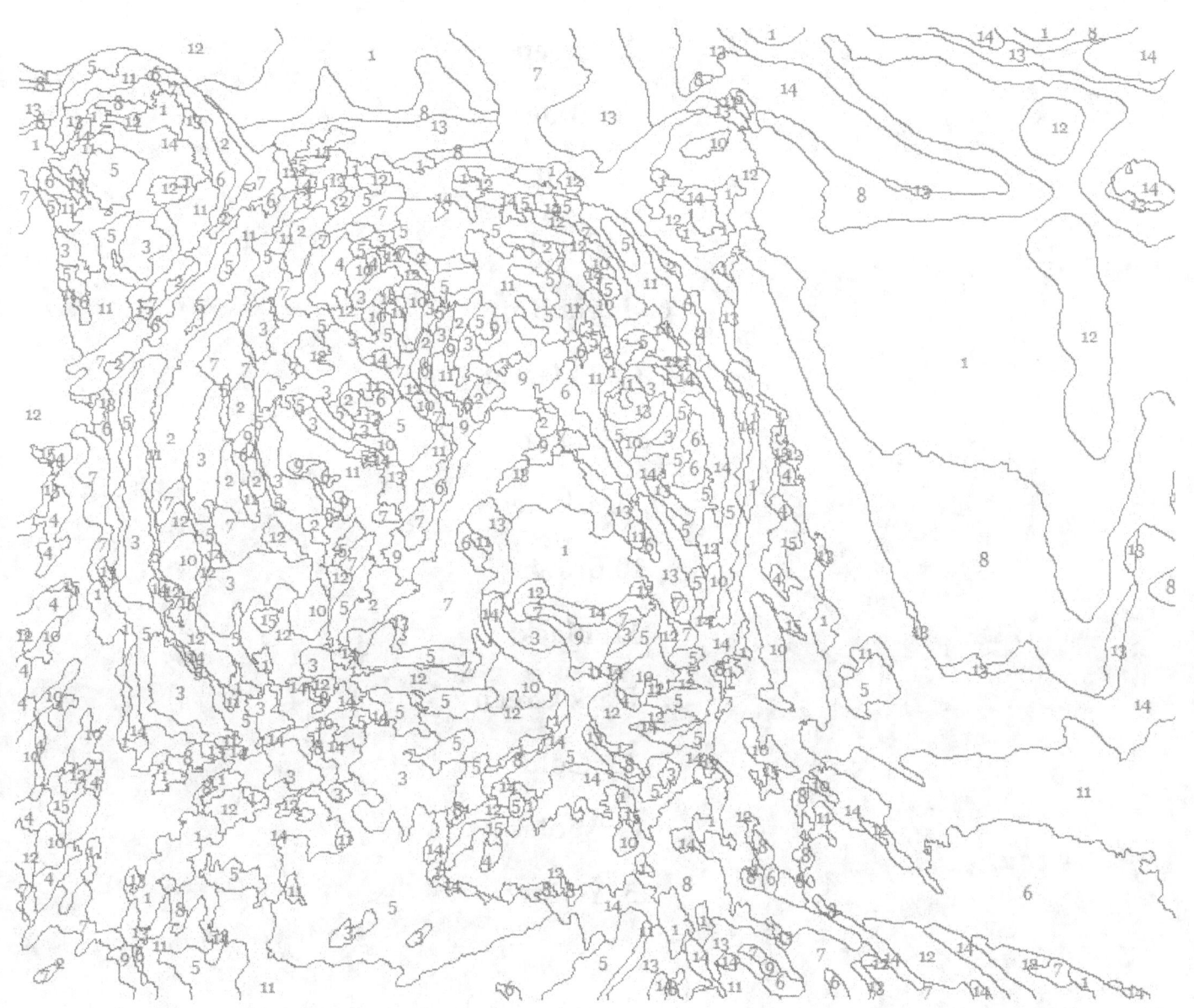

1. Red

2. Green

3. Blue

4. Pink

5. Purple

6. Light Blue

7. Light Green

8. Orange

9. Dark Red

10. Brown

11. Black

12. Dark Green

13. Gold

14. Violet

15. Yellow

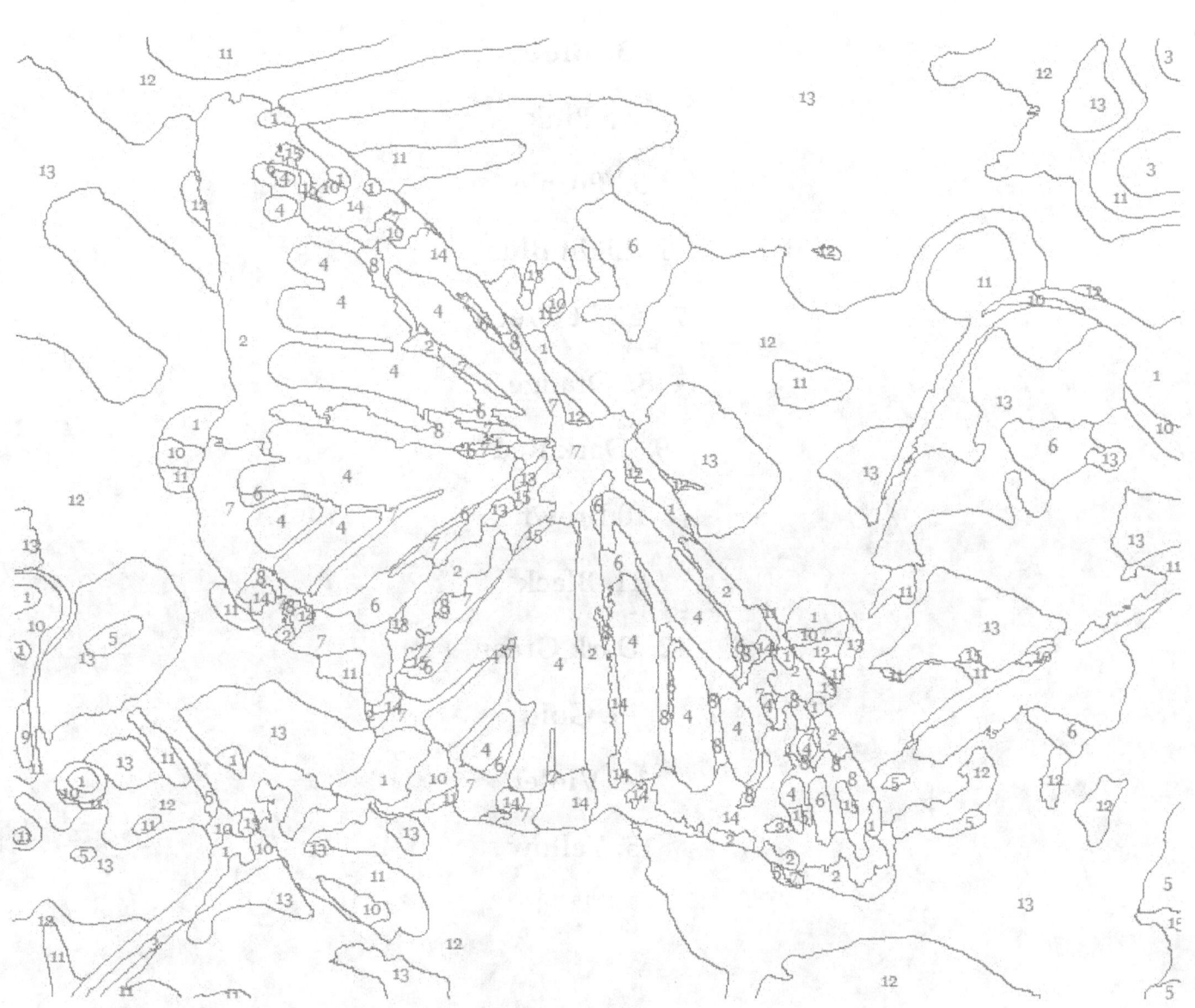

1. Red

2. Green

3. Blue

4. Pink

5. Purple

6. Light Blue

7. Light Green

8. Orange

9. Dark Red

10. Brown

11. Black

12. Dark Green

13. Gold

14. Violet

15. Yellow

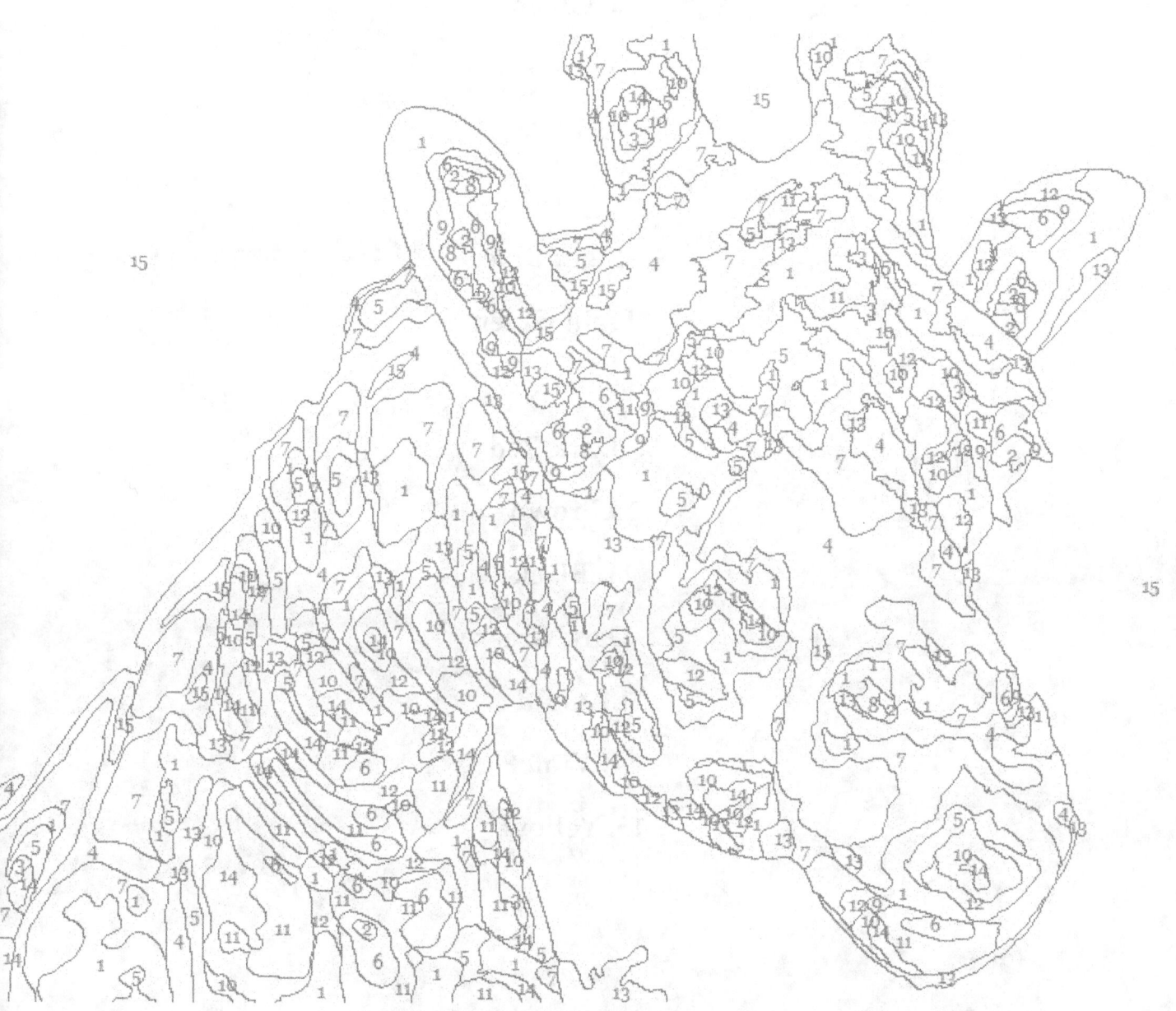

1. Red

2. Green

3. Blue

4. Pink

5. Purple

6. Light Blue

7. Light Green

8. Orange

9. Dark Red

10. Brown

11. Black

12. Dark Green

13. Gold

14. Violet

15. Yellow

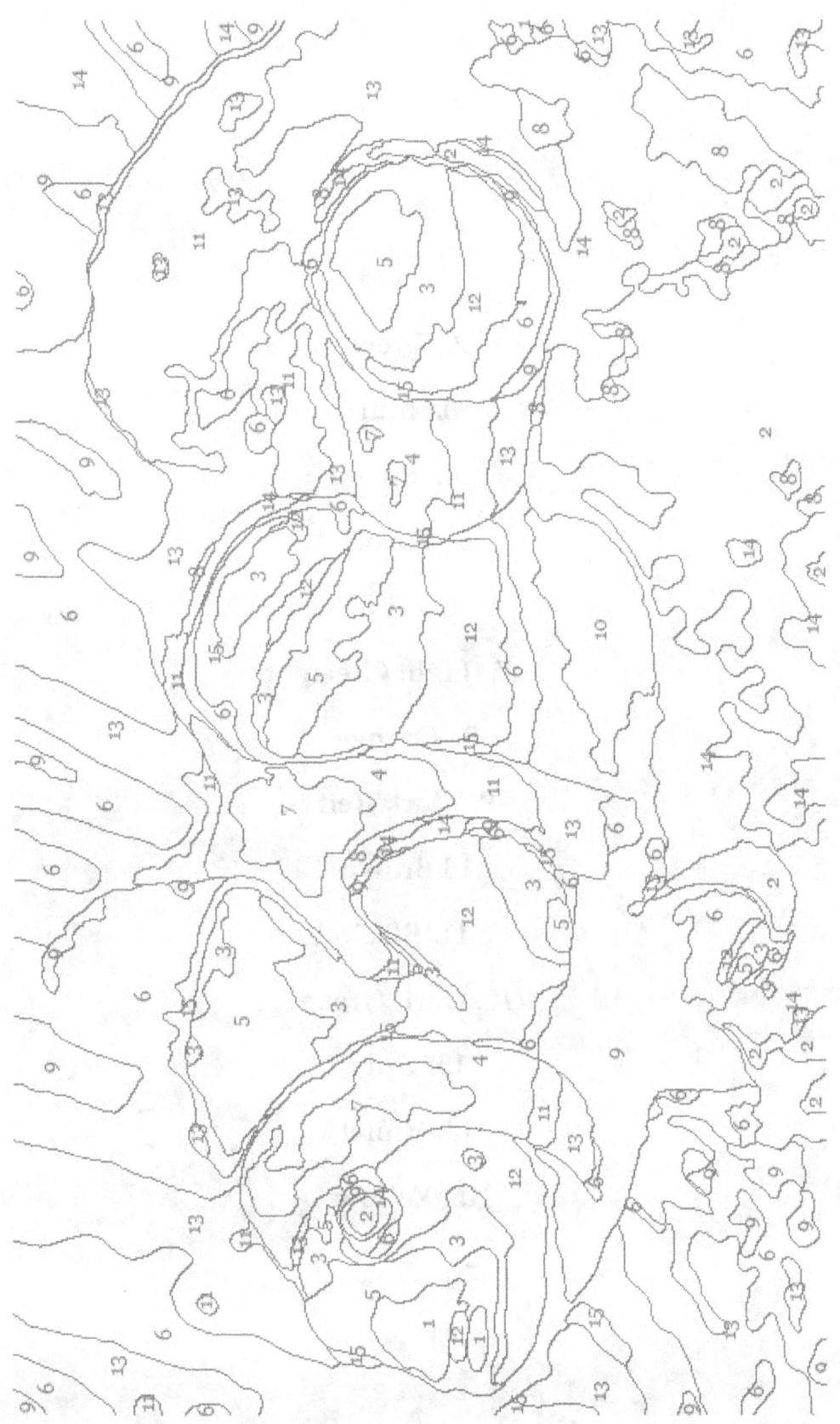

1. Red

2. Green

3. Blue

4. Pink

5. Purple

6. Light Blue

7. Light Green

8. Orange

9. Dark Red

10. Brown

11. Black

12. Dark Green

13. Gold

14. Violet

15. Yellow

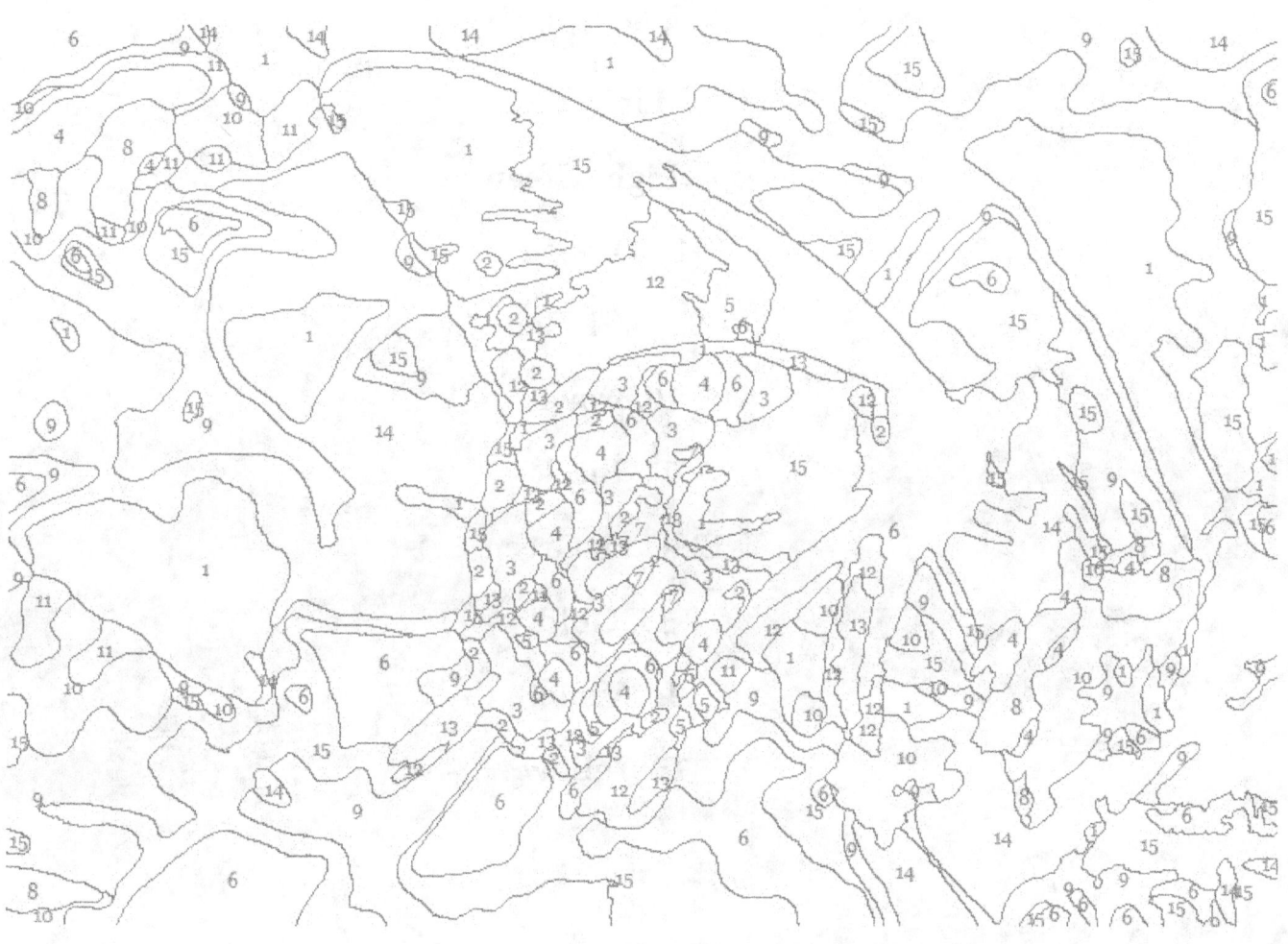

1. Red

2. Green

3. Blue

4. Pink

5. Purple

6. Light Blue

7. Light Green

8. Orange

9. Dark Red

10. Brown

11. Black

12. Dark Green

13. Gold

14. Violet

15. Yellow

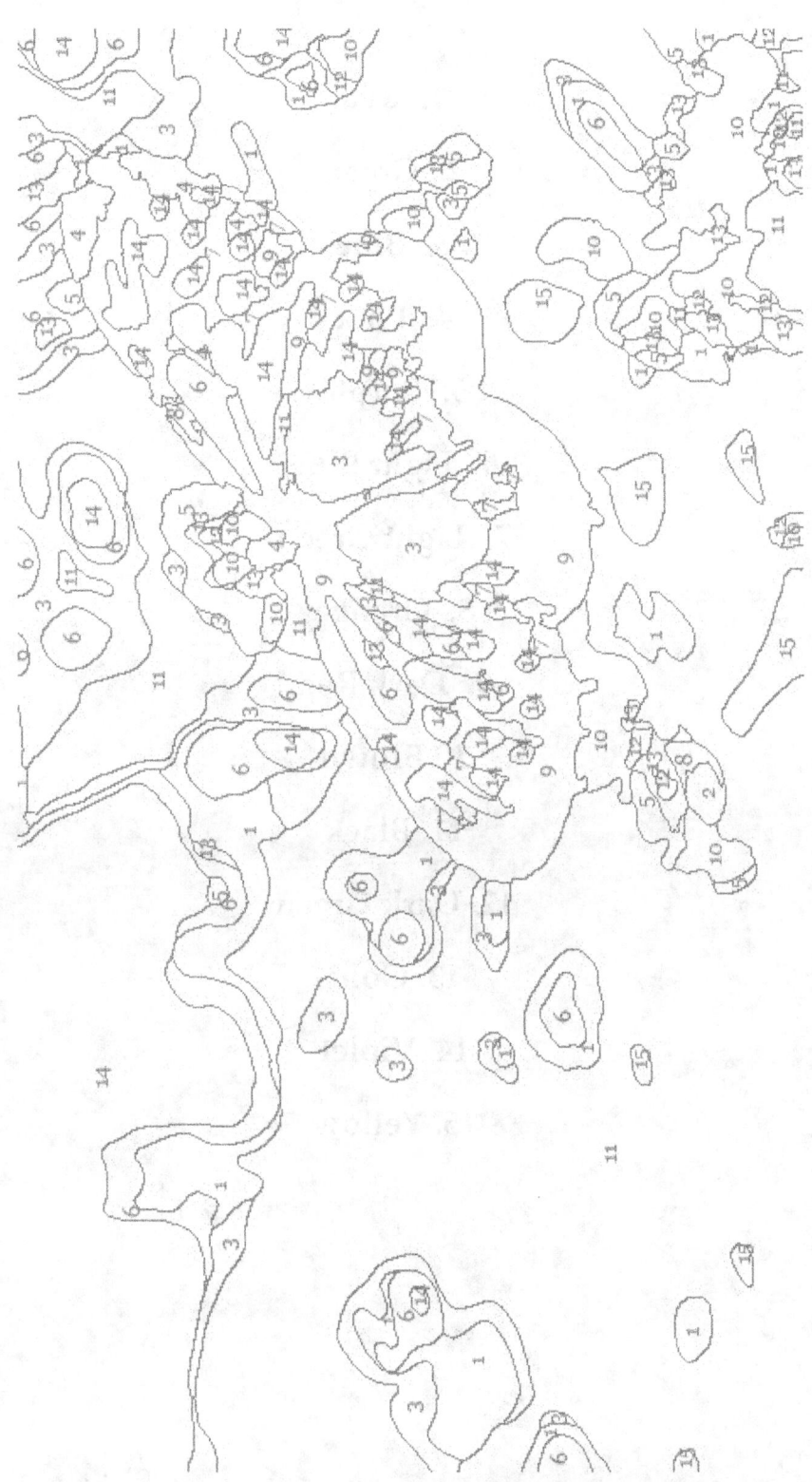

1. Red

2. Green

3. Blue

4. Pink

5. Purple

6. Light Blue

7. Light Green

8. Orange

9. Dark Red

10. Brown

11. Black

12. Dark Green

13. Gold

14. Violet

15. Yellow

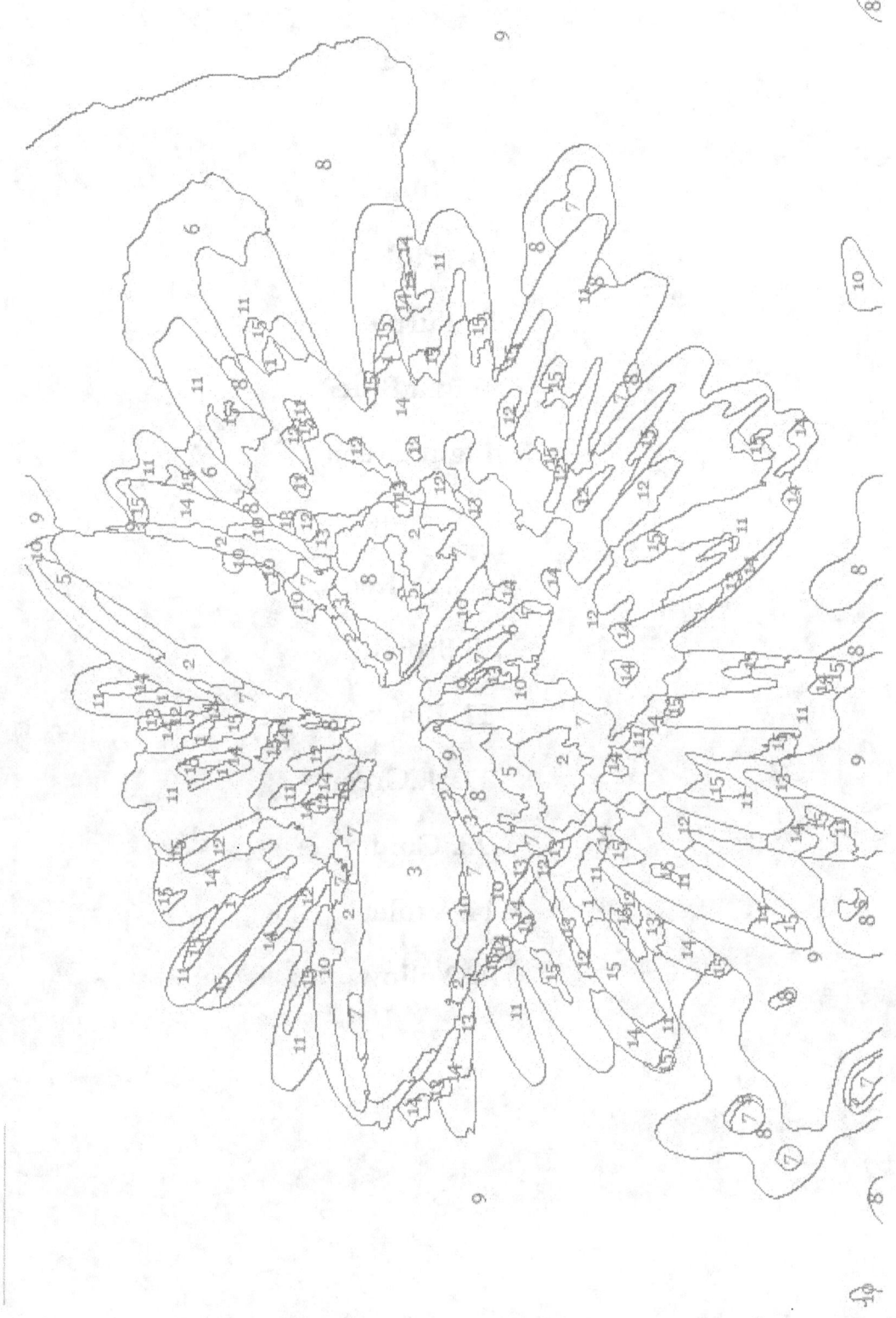

1. Red

2. Green

3. Blue

4. Pink

5. Purple

6. Light Blue

7. Light Green

8. Orange

9. Dark Red

10. Brown

11. Black

12. Dark Green

13. Gold

14. Violet

15. Yellow

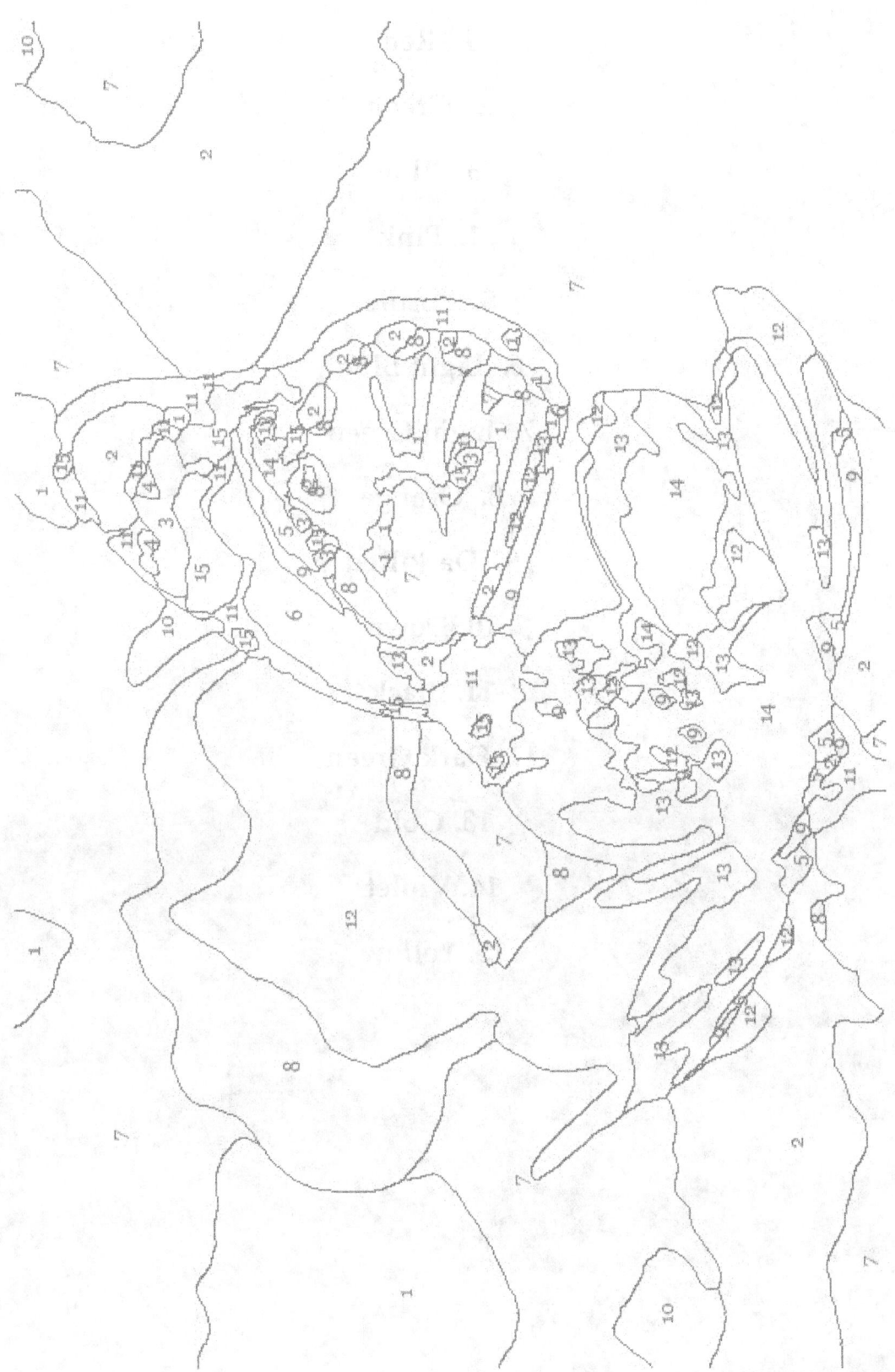

1. Red

2. Green

3. Blue

4. Pink

5. Purple

6. Light Blue

7. Light Green

8. Orange

9. Dark Red

10. Brown

11. Black

12. Dark Green

13. Gold

14. Violet

15. Yellow